EXIS

Less of an orientation and more a way of understanding of being human, existential therapy draws on rich and diverse philosophical traditions and ways of viewing the world. Traditionally it has been seen as difficult to summarise and comprehend, and the air of mystery surrounding existential ideas has been exacerbated by the dense language often used by philosophers and practitioners. *Existential Therapy: 100 Key Points and Techniques* provides a comprehensive and accessible guide to a fascinating and exciting body of knowledge, and the therapeutic approach it informs. Divided into five parts the topics covered include:

- Existentialism – inception to present day
- Theoretical assumptions
- Existential phenomenological therapy in practice
- Ethics and existential therapy
- Bringing it all together.

Existential Therapy: 100 Key Points and Techniques will be essential reading for all trainee and qualified counsellors, psychotherapists, psychologists and psychiatrists who want to use the wisdom of existential ideas in their work with clients. It will also benefit clients and potential clients who want to find out how existential ideas and existential therapy can help them explore what it means to be alive.

Susan Iacovou is an existential psychotherapist working in online education for the University of Derby Online and in private practice in Cheshire. She manages a range of university programmes in psychology and psychotherapy and has developed award-winning teaching materials for over 100 organisations worldwide. Susan Iacovou has been published widely and this is her fourth book.

Karen Weixel-Dixon is a psychotherapist, supervisor, and accredited mediator in private practice, and a visiting lecturer at Regent's University London. She is co-director for Re-Solution partnership. She has been published widely.

100 Key Points and Techniques
Series Editor: Windy Dryden

ALSO IN THIS SERIES:

COGNITIVE THERAPY: 100 KEY POINTS AND TECHNIQUES
Michael Neenan and Windy Dryden

RATIONAL EMOTIVE BEHAVIOUR THERAPY: 100 KEY POINTS AND TECHNIQUES
Windy Dryden and Michael Neenan

FAMILY THERAPY: 100 KEY POINTS AND TECHNIQUES
Mark Rivett and Eddy Street

TRANSACTIONAL ANALYSIS: 100 KEY POINTS AND TECHNIQUES
Mark Widdowson

PERSON-CENTRED THERAPY: 100 KEY POINTS
Paul Wilkins

GESTALT THERAPY: 100 KEY POINTS AND TECHNIQUES
Dave Mann

INTEGRATIVE THERAPY: 100 KEY POINTS AND TECHNIQUES
Maria Gilbert and Vanja Orlans

SOLUTION FOCUSED BRIEF THERAPY: 100 KEY POINTS AND TECHNIQUES
Harvey Ratner, Evan George and Chris Iveson

COGNITIVE BEHAVIOUR THERAPY: 100 KEY POINTS AND TECHNIQUES, 2ND EDITION
Michael Neenan and Windy Dryden

RATIONAL EMOTIVE BEHAVIOUR THERAPY: 100 KEY POINTS AND TECHNIQUES, 2ND EDITION
Windy Dryden and Michael Neenan

EXISTENTIAL THERAPY: 100 KEY POINTS AND TECHNIQUES
Susan Iacovou and Karen Weixel-Dixon

EXISTENTIAL THERAPY

100 KEY POINTS AND TECHNIQUES

Susan Iacovou and Karen Weixel-Dixon

Routledge
Taylor & Francis Group
LONDON AND NEW YORK

First published 2015
by Routledge
27 Church Road, Hove, East Sussex, BN3 2FA

and by Routledge
711 Third Avenue, New York, NY 10017

Routledge is an imprint of the Taylor & Francis Group, an informa business

British Library Cataloguing in Publication Data
A catalogue record for this book is available from the British Library

Library of Congress Cataloging in Publication Data
Iacovou, Susan (Psychotherapist)
Existential therapy : 100 key points and techniques / Susan Iacovou and Karen Weixel-Dixon. -- Dual First.
pages cm
Includes bibliographical references and index.
ISBN 978-0-415-64441-9 (hbk : alk. paper) -- ISBN 978-0-415-64442-6 (pbk : alk. paper) -- ISBN 978-1-315-70926-0 (ebk) 1. Existential psychotherapy. I. Weixel-Dixon, Karen. II. Title.
RC489.E93I23 2015
616.89'14--dc23
2014042673

ISBN: 978-0-415-64441-9 (hbk)
ISBN: 978-0-415-64442-6 (pbk)
ISBN: 978-1-315-70926-0 (ebk)

Typeset in Aldus LT Std
by Saxon Graphics Ltd, Derby

To our clients, from whom we learn courage, resilience and bloody mindedness

To the teachers who remind us that convictions are more dangerous enemies of truth than lies

And, of course, to our families, who see us at our best and at our worst and still love us

"A very quick guide to existential therapy, which will help you get your head around some complex philosophical terms and issues in a clear and straightforward way."

Professor Emmy van Deurzen,
Principal of the New School of Psychotherapy
and Counselling.

"As a clinician who has taught existential therapy to mental health professionals and graduate students for the past twenty-five years, I have long wished for a book that would provide both an introduction and a sophisticated, non-simplistic look at existential therapy. This is not an easy task, considering the complexity of existential philosophy and the varieties of existential therapy. Susan Iacovou and Karen Weixel-Dixon have contributed just such a book. Well-written, accessible, and not full of philosophical jargon, their book makes the sometimes esoteric world of existential therapy accessible to a wide range of readers. Anyone wanting to gain an overview of existential theory and therapy would do well to start with this book. It can be returned to again and again as one gains a greater knowledge of the field and wishes to review its key concepts and practices. I would recommend it to both beginners and experienced therapists of all orientations. It should also prove to be of interested to general readers seeking an alternative to the scientistic technique-driven approaches that often dominate contemporary psychotherapy."

Betty Cannon, Ph.D.,
author of *Sartre and Psychoanalysis,*
Director of the Boulder Psychotherapy Institute (Colorado),
& founder of Applied Existential Psychotherapy (AEP).

"A super contribution to the field. Comprehensive, expertly-informed and laying out existential thought and practice in a highly accessible, engaging, and applicable way."

Mick Cooper,
author of *Existential psychotherapy and counselling: Contributions to a pluralistic practice* (Sage, 2015),
Professor of Counselling Psychology, University of Roehampton.

CONTENTS

FOREWORD

This book is part of a series, edited by Professor Windy Dryden and published by Routledge, designed to educate the mental health professional, the trainee mental health professional, the client and the downright curious as to the key tools and techniques involved in particular orientations or flavours of psychotherapy. This particular book originated from the first author's desire to share the powerful and unique insights offered by existential psychotherapy with all those who share an interest in philosophy, psychology, psychotherapy and what it means to be human. It emerged as the book you see now from the experiences, beliefs and worldviews of both authors, which in turn were heavily influenced by the inspirational and visionary ideas of so many philosophers and practitioners that we lack the space and words to acknowledge each of them personally.

Nothing contained in this book is true. For there is no truth – only truths as we uniquely perceive them. Our only hope as authors is that *our* truths have some impact on the worldviews of you, our readers, and in turn upon the lives of the individuals with whom you live, work and play. There is no formula for life, and accordingly there is no formula for the therapeutic endeavour. Use this book to question what you know, to inform whom you seek to be and, if all else fails, to prop open the door that keeps blowing closed in the breeze.

ABOUT THE AUTHORS

Susan Iacovou is an existential therapist and counselling psychologist with a private practice in Cheshire. She has published widely, most recently co-editing the ground-breaking text *Existential Perspectives on Relationship Therapy* with Emmy van Deurzen. Susan is an expert in online learning and manages online counselling, psychology and science undergraduate and postgraduate programmes for the University of Derby Online Learning. She received an MA in Psychology from Edinburgh University and more recently completed her Doctorate in Existential Counselling and Psychology with the New School of Psychotherapy and Counselling.

Karen Weixel-Dixon is a psychotherapist, mediator, supervisor and trainer in the fields of psychotherapy, mediation and coaching. Her paradigm is described as existential-phenomenological and she has a special interest in how people engage with temporality. She maintains practices and delivers seminars in the UK and in France, her current country of residence.

INTRODUCTION

Our aim in writing this book is threefold: to introduce existential therapy as it can be practised; to give therapists/mental health practitioners from other theoretical backgrounds an insight into how the basic assumptions of existential therapy might enhance their practices; and to offer anyone seeking to explore their way of being in the world a starting point from which to do so.

Existential therapy has a long tradition, based upon centuries of philosophical debate around what it means to be human. Many books on existentialism are lengthy and difficult to comprehend, reflecting the complexity of existence and the many and disparate views that have been taken on its challenges. As authors, our ambition was to represent the breadth and depth of existential ideas and the invaluable insights they offer the therapeutic endeavour, but also to provide readers with an accessible and practical route into the use of these ideas in a therapeutic setting. This has not been an easy task. At times we have had to simplify, often brutally, the core philosophical concepts being presented; at other times we have had to construct an overly rigid representation of how these concepts translate into therapeutic practice.

Ultimately this book is not a comprehensive theoretical treatise, nor does it represent the myriad ways in which existential therapy can be practised. Readers are encouraged to use it as an introductory guide to the philosophy behind, and practice of, existential therapy: as a doorway to further reading and exploration.

Existential therapy doesn't have at its base a theory of psychology designed to explain and treat human distress. It is difficult therefore for us to present a guide to existential therapy in a logical manner from start to finish. Existential therapy, by virtue of its focus on the unique nature of every individual and of every human encounter, is resistant to any attempt to translate its ideas into systems, methodologies, tools and techniques. Readers will find that they need to be content to learn about existential therapy without an overarching plan to guide them. Our hope is that by building up your knowledge of the individual bricks you will get to a point at which you can build a coherent whole of your own. This is essentially what the existential therapist does – as Cooper (2003) points out, there are as many existential therapies as there are existential therapists.

We have tried to make each section of the book self-standing, but because of the highly inter-related nature of many of the core concepts, this has resulted in some crossover in a few areas. Where this is the case, we have taken the opportunity to illustrate the reappearing concept differently, in order to add something new to the reader's understanding.

Ultimately, existential therapy is a *way of being with* a client, not *a way of doing* things for or to a client. It is a therapy that is co-created each time by therapist and client. It cannot easily be summarised or explained and resists definition and measurement. Yet for those willing to ask the fundamental questions about the human situation, it offers something pure and of permanent value.

Part 1

EXISTENTIALISM – INCEPTION TO PRESENT DAY

This section of the book briefly introduces existentialism and existential therapy and highlights the central role existential ideas play in modern life today.

1

WHAT IS EXISTENTIALISM?

Many people have heard the term 'existentialism' and some may have some vague notions as to what it refers to. It may, for example, conjure up pictures of Gauloise-smoking philosophers in French cafés, or poets and playwrights producing pessimistic and melancholic reflections on what it means to be human. Some may associate it with amorality or despair, or consider it to be the stuff of academia, with little relevance to the everyday. In fact, the contributions made by existential thinkers to philosophy, art, literature, science and numerous other fields are immeasurable, and existentialism offers those who care to explore it access to the collective wisdom of many of humanity's greatest thinkers

Perhaps one of the reasons why existentialism evades common understanding is that it resists concise definition. There are a number of reasons why this is the case. First, existentialism isn't a unitary, coordinated body of knowledge – indeed, for every apparently central tenet identified as existential an equally strongly held but opposing view is readily presented and hotly debated. On the subject of faith, for example, we have Kaufman and Nietzsche (1974) declaring God is dead, while Tillich (2000) exhorts us to have faith and turn to the infinite. Second, many contradictory attempts are made to define existentialism according to a particular time period, often talking about it as a 'twentieth-century cultural movement' or as 'having mid-nineteenth-century origins but coming of age in the twentieth century', yet existentialism without Nietzsche (1844–1900) and Kierkegaard (1813–1855), to name but two, would be unthinkable. Indeed, existential themes can be found in the works of Aristotle and Plato, in the Old Testament, in 'The Epic of Gilgamesh' (Jastrow & Clay,

2010) and in the teachings of Buddha. Finally, to add to the confusion, many philosophers and writers defined today as existentialists – Camus and Heidegger, for example – resisted being defined as such while still alive.

There are definitions of existentialism that focus on what it is *not*, or what it is opposed to. Many see it as a counter to the traditional philosophy and rationalism of the Enlightenment, as seen in the works of Descartes and Spinoza. (Indeed, Crowell (2010) argues that existentialism is a general approach to rejecting other systematic philosophies rather than being a systematic philosophy in itself.) Others describe it as a reaction against arbitrary social values and institutions such as organised religion, and their attempts to control individual thought and behaviour. However, these negative definitions do nothing to tell us what existentialism actually *is*, anymore than describing punk music as 'not rock' or 'not jazz' helps us to understand what 'God Save the Queen' by the Sex Pistols actually sounds like.

It is possible to discern some core areas of concern that are central to most, if not all, existential philosophies and, through these, to establish in broad terms a working definition of existentialism on which to base the rest of this book.

Ultimately existentialism concerns itself simply with what it is to exist as a human being. It is a philosophical approach to understanding our experiences, our world, our relationships and this thing we call our 'self'. It doesn't deny the validity of natural science, but makes the point that human beings cannot be fully understood in terms of it. Human existence can be understood only through a thorough examination of our experience of what it means *to be* (Heidegger, 1978) and through an understanding of the universal issues we face in being human, including freedom, responsibility, meaning, isolation, death and anxiety. It's about life and its challenges. It's about us as individuals and as beings in relation to others. It's about how we navigate our journeys from birth to death. It's about all that we are, and all we might be. Existentialism is, quite simply, about being human. And existential psychotherapy, as this book will reveal, is about exploring each individual client's experience of what it is to be human in all its complexity.

2

HISTORICAL BACKGROUND, PHILOSOPHICAL FOUNDATIONS

The roots of existential therapy lie in 3,000 years of philosophy and, in particular, in the human quest to understand life and overcome adversity (Deurzen, 2007). These roots encompass the wisdom of the Ancient Greeks, incorporating tenets of Eastern philosophies such as Buddhism and Taoism and taking inspiration from the work of an eclectic mix of philosophers, writers, artists and theologians. However, there are two strands of thought that have most heavily influenced the development of existential therapy – the diverse field of work that is known collectively as existential philosophy, and the philosophy of phenomenology, which seeks to determine how we experience the world.

EXISTENTIAL PHILOSOPHY

Although he never used the term existential, the Danish philosopher Kierkegaard is widely regarded as the 'father of existentialism' and, along with Nietzsche, as the precursor of existentialism as a movement. Kierkegaard was one of the first philosophers to focus his work on the exploration of angst, despair, love and the universal contradictions of human 'existence', while Nietzsche talked about the importance of individuality, attacking conventional systems of morality and power and encouraging people to live with passion.

The first person to use the term existential to describe a particular philosophical approach is thought to be French philosopher Gabriel Marcel (1949). The word was then adopted by Jean-Paul Sartre and became associated with his literary and philosophical work and with that of his long-term partner Simone de Beauvoir and fellow French philosophers Maurice Merleau-Ponty and Albert Camus. Latterly the work of German philosophers Jaspers, Heidegger and Buber was incorporated under this banner, along with that of the Romanian Ionescu and Americans Tillich and May. On the back of the work of these (and other) philosophers and writers, existential philosophy flourished across mid-twentieth-century Europe. Taking root in the imagination of people ravaged by the horror of two world wars, it was a philosophy that emphasised human individuality, freedom and responsibility, and encouraged resistance to systems of thought that sought to control, or to reduce the complexity of human existence to a set of laws, rules or statistics (Cooper, 2003).

PHENOMENOLOGY

The other central strand of existential therapy is phenomenology. Often described as a study of things as they appear, phenomenology was originally developed by the German mathematician Edmund Husserl (1859–1958). Husserl rejected the idea that truth was to be found solely in objective, natural science and instead proposed a method of studying human experience that acknowledged both the objective and the subjective. He recognised the fact that we are participant-observers in the world – we cannot stand outside of the world, and therefore, when we talk about something, we cannot help but talk about it through the lens of our experience of it (Adams, 2013). What phenomenology aims to do is reveal things as they actually are by studying them in a way that removes the assumptions and preconceptions that limit our understanding of them.

EXISTENTIAL THERAPY

Existential and phenomenological ideas went on to influence a number of fields, including theology (through the work of people like Paul Tillich and Karl Barth), psychiatry (through the world of Ludwig Binswanger, Medard Boss and more recently Ronnie Laing), sociology (through the work of people like Jacques Derrida and Michel Foucault) and psychology (through Otto Rank, Victor Frankl and Rollo May, for example). Most significantly for the purposes of this book, existentialism has been applied to the field of psychotherapy. Existential psychotherapies, including Daseinsanalysis, Logotherapy, and the therapies that make up the American and British schools of existential therapy, each bring their own particular blend of ideas from existential philosophy and phenomenology and present credible alternatives to therapies based on the dominant medical model of mental health. And as we will see later on in this book, existential therapy need not be practised to the exclusion of other types of therapy, but rather has something to offer practitioners from a very wide range of other schools.

3

THE BASIS OF AN EXISTENTIAL APPROACH TO THERAPY

Unlike other forms of psychotherapy, which take their inspiration primarily from psychology or medicine, existential therapy is philosophy-based. This doesn't mean that it is heavily theoretical (in fact, it is arguably less theory-driven than many other forms of therapy). Nor does it ignore the psychological, emotional or behavioural in favour of esoteric allusions, or involve the therapist and client in endless philosophical debates about the meaning of life or the existence of a higher being. Existential therapy is *informed by*, not focused on, philosophy (primarily – but not exclusively – existential philosophy) and benefits from the wisdom, insight and perspicacity it offers.

The existential therapist recognises that we all face certain universal conditions and that the differences between us come down to how we choose to respond to these conditions. For example, we will all ultimately face our own death – but some of us choose to meet this reality head-on, grabbing any opportunities to truly live in the meantime, while others try to deny their mortality, spending vast amounts of money on products and procedures to help them retain at least the appearance of youth.

Existential therapy focuses on this uniqueness – resisting the tendency to place people in boxes or typologies according, for example, to their personality, age, gender, educational background, behaviour, sexual preferences, political views or choice of lifestyle. It is therefore a 'non-pathologising' therapy, in which a very wide range of human thought, behaviour and emotion is considered normal, and where terms like 'diagnosis', 'illness' and 'symptoms' and the medical model of mental health are seen as largely unnecessary and potentially harmful, restricting both our understanding of their world and the sense of responsibility and freedom with which we approach our challenges.

Existential therapy offers both therapist and client an opportunity to discover how the client chooses to express their individuality. It's about clarifying their worldview, their values and beliefs, and the attitude they take to their world, and to the people and events they encounter. Illuminating these stances leaves the client free to consider whether or not these ways of being, thinking, feeling and behaving will best help them live a life in line with their values, a life that is meaningful, a life in which they engage actively with the choices they make and strive to make them in light of their own needs and the needs of others.

The existential therapist recognises that we are good at deceiving ourselves and that this ability to rationalise, ignore or underestimate the significance of evidence that contradicts what we want to believe can often make us strangers to ourselves, standing in the way of our ability to truly know our reality. As a result, we may refuse to see how we, or other people, are contributing to our unhappiness, distress or lack of fulfilment, perhaps because we are frightened of what we might lose, or how we might have to change if we were to open our eyes.

An existential therapist accepts these strategies as ways of dealing with life and living, and approaches each client's story with curiosity. Clients are invited to describe and examine their behaviours, relationships, thoughts and ideas and encouraged to be open to those alternative ways of thinking, behaving and being that they are not currently choosing.

Existential therapy is not necessarily about major change (though for many clients it leads to new and profound ways of being). A client may decide to make some, or even many, changes in their life, or they may decide not to make any outward changes at all. Often the inward changes in emotions, attitudes and ideas are enough to allow them to move forward and deal with any challenges they are facing.

Although existential ideas are relevant to everybody, existential therapy is not a flavour of therapy that everyone finds palatable (Tantam, 2002). It demands much of clients, who must be prepared to wrestle with, and ultimately come to accept, the dilemmas and paradoxes of human existence, to take responsibility for the choices they make (and the consequences that result from them) and to confront absurdity, meaninglessness and the finitude of their own existence with courage and tenacity.

4

EXISTENTIAL THERAPY HERE AND NOW

Over the last ten years, the number of schools of existential therapy around the world, together with the number of practising existential therapists, has grown rapidly. At the time of writing, the first World Congress for Existential Therapy is being planned and will take place in London in 2015. The venue for this event reflects the continuing dominance of the British School of Existential Therapy in the development and promotion of existential theory and practice (Cooper, 2012). Historically in the UK, concepts from existential philosophy were first incorporated into the care of those with mental health problems by Laing and Cooper, who opened therapeutic communities offering refuge to those who wanted to deal with their mental health issues without the involvement of the medical establishment (Laing, 1960, 1961; Laing & Cooper, 1964; Cooper, 1967). Psychologist and psychotherapist Emmy van Deurzen, who worked briefly with Laing, went on to establish the first school of existential therapy in London, and now leads The New School of Psychotherapy and Counselling, offering existentially oriented programmes in counselling, psychology and coaching. Van Deurzen's work (Deurzen, 2009, 2012; Deurzen & Adams, 2010; Deurzen & Iacovou, 2013), together with that of Ernesto Spinelli (Spinelli, 2005, 2006, 2007), who has worked separately but contemporaneously to van Deurzen, resulted in the consolidation of existential ideas into a coherent therapeutic approach in Britain. There are now a number of training schools providing courses in existential therapy, and many others that include existential therapy in their curricula. The Society for Existential Analysis publishes a bi-annual *Journal of Existential Analysis*, and a thriving conference and workshop programme on existential topics encourages therapists from all orientations to incorporate existential ideas into their practices.

Further afield, the International Federation for Daseinanalysis (a form of existential therapy influenced by the philosophy of Martin Heidegger (Heidegger, 1978)) represents existential therapists from a number of countries around the world, including Canada, Greece, Switzerland, Austria and Brazil. An International Society for Existential Analysis also exists and has members in 19 countries, on four continents. In Europe, two forms of existential therapy dominate – Daseinanalysis and Logotherapy (a meaning-focused existential therapy developed by Victor Frankl (Frankl, 2004)). In the United States, existential-humanistic therapy is preeminent, largely because of the popularity of its leading proponent – psychiatrist, psychotherapist and novelist Victor Yalom (2006, 2011). Existential therapies are also gaining ground in South America (Toledo, 2011), Canada (Wong, 2013), Australia (Strasser & Strasser, 1997) and Russia (Leontiev, 2013).

There are many challenges facing existential therapists today – including how to explain and teach an approach that has been inspired by such a diverse range of thought, and that takes an epistemological stance that resists systematisation, indeed considers it to be the antithesis of good practice. And yet existential ideas are arguably becoming more and more relevant in a modern world, where people live at an increasingly fast pace and are encouraged to surround themselves with 'things' as part of the frantic pursuit of the happiness and pleasure they have come to see as their right. In this environment, a therapy that offers to help people deal with feelings of meaninglessness and emptiness, and gives them courage to face adversity and enables them to live life authentically, in line with their values, can only become more relevant.

Part 2

THEORETICAL ASSUMPTIONS

In this part of the book we introduce you to the key theoretical ideas that underpin existential therapy. What you will realise as you read through or dip in and out of this section is that existential theory need not be dense and incomprehensible (despite its reputation, and the best efforts of some of its proponents!). Stripped of its occasionally academic and forbidding exterior, its immediate relevance to the therapeutic endeavour is illuminated.

5

EXISTENCE AND ESSENCE AND THE CONCEPT OF SELF

If asked to describe themselves, most people would pause for thought but would quite quickly be able to say a bit about who they were, the work they did, their likes and dislikes, how many children they had, and so on. The question 'Who are you?' makes sense to us, and the assumption behind the question is that it also makes sense to talk about ourselves as though we are consistent, perhaps even fixed, beings with particular personalities, outlooks and habits. When Sartre asserts that existence precedes essence, however, he is pointing out that this is not the case.

Sartre reminds us that we exist in the world before we actually become anything. And our existence is a 'verb-like process' (Cooper, 2012, p14) or what Merleau-Ponty (1962) describes as a flux. We are experiential beings, constantly interacting with the world. Only by choosing to be, think or do certain things do we begin to create a 'self'. But we are still not immutable entities with set personalities, abilities and ways of seeing the world. Rather, we are continuously in a process of 'becoming'. Every choice we make, every action we take, every interaction with another person or another object, changes us in one way or another so that we are never static (Spinelli (2007) calls this dynamic flow of experience *worlding*). We may choose to make sense of the world, and of others, and ourselves, through imposing an element of constancy, but this is a convenient illusion, and something that we mustn't accept blindly. The most we can say is that we have a coherent *sense of self* (Adams, 2013) that, to some extent at least, remains consistent over time.

The exciting thing about Sartre's assertion, if we accept it, is that it opens up the possibility of change – in other words, it has the potential to liberate us from aspects of our identity that no longer serve us. A counselling client might say something like 'I'm a loner/joker/intellectual/extrovert', or 'That's just how I am' as though they were a fixed object like a table or a chair, with permanent, unchanging characteristics. Other people in the client's life may reinforce these views – 'My mother says I was born shy'; 'My wife laughs when I tell her I never used to lose my temper so easily.' An existential counsellor will encourage her clients to question both their own and others' tendency to objectify the client in this way. She will invite them to explore the possibility of a more flexible self-concept, encouraging them to take responsibility for deciding for themselves who they are at any particular moment.

The existential practitioner will also help their clients to recognise the limitations or drawbacks of this freedom. There is an ongoing tension between our need for stability and our need for flexibility, both in ourselves and in others. While the potential exists for us to be many different people, some element of constancy is necessary if we are to function in the world and in relationships with others. If we allow ourselves to become too fixed, we become dull and predictable – stuck in our ways, unable to respond to our environment. If, on the other hand, we don't impose any constancy upon ourselves, we will become confused, our moods, preferences and behaviours dangerously unpredictable. If we see others as fixed and unchanging we will quickly become complacent about who they are and what they need from us, and may be surprised, even horrified, when they want something different. Alternatively, by refusing to accept some of the more persistent characteristics in others, we may find ourselves trying to change them; resulting in them feeling unacceptable or not good enough.

6

BEING-IN-THE-WORLD

'Being-in-the-world' is a term created by Heidegger (1978) to describe what it is to be human. Also known as 'Dasein' in the literature, the hyphenated format of Heidegger's term is designed to provoke us into re-thinking ideas we may have taken for granted – in this case, the idea that we are somehow separate and distinct from the world around us.

Being-in-the-world is a term that makes it clear that we are always situated within the world, involved in a meaningful context consisting of people, ideas, places, objects and events – inter-connected and inter-dependent. While we might on occasion seek or even long to be apart from this context, the very fact that we feel this way implies a relationship between ourselves and the world: we may choose isolation, but there remains a 'what' from which we are trying to separate ourselves. Even the hermit, hiding away in his cave and shunning the world, is still hiding from something.

As a consequence of this connectedness to the world, we cannot stand over or outside our situation and judge it objectively. This is a difficult concept for some clients to accept. Faced with anxiety or sadness, in the midst of emotional turmoil, it can be comforting for them to conclude that if they could only see their situation objectively, things would improve. Heidegger sometimes used the term 'dwelling' to make the point that we don't merely occupy a particular physical space in the world, but rather we are in a familiar place in it – a place where we make sense of our world through the subjective lens of our values, ideas and experiences in it. Polt (1999) suggested the term 'amid' to describe the way we are always situated amidst meanings and purposes.

This concept of 'being-in-the-world' has important implications for psychotherapy as it reminds us that we are never able to understand our lives in isolation, without considering the world around us and the ways that we connect to it. Existential therapists work with their clients to examine and gently question the ways in which they are actively engaged in the world, and with the particulars of their environment. Clients are encouraged to explicitly acknowledge their modes of engagement with the people, places, ideas, cultures and objects that make up their world. The alternative is to exist in 'everydayness', taking for granted the significance (or lack of significance) they accord to what they encounter. After all, everything that we encounter has some sort of significance for us: we 'care' about the elements in our world (Heidegger, 1962). Even if we deem an aspect of our world to be unimportant or irrelevant, we have still had to evaluate that aspect in order to determine its insignificance. Existential therapy offers the opportunity to explicitly examine these evaluations and their implications for the way we see the world. A client who views the behaviour of his partner through the lens of his experience with his abusive mother, for example, may categorise many of his experiences in the relationship as 'normal' and may fail to acknowledge their impact upon him. Exploring the implications of viewing his relationship through alternative lenses may highlight a range of other possible interpretations and actions.

7

BEING-IN-THE-WORLD-WITH-OTHERS

A corollary of being-in-the-world is being-in-the-world-with-others (Heidegger, 1978). Although this is another Heideggerian phrase, the idea it refers to is one that other existential philosophers have debated widely (Husserl, 1931) and have described variously as 'inter-subjectivity' or 'relatedness'.

Whatever term we use, the concept behind 'being-in-the-world-with-others' is a straightforward one and focuses on the idea that human existence is characteristically and essentially relational and something we cannot escape – any attempt at isolation or total separateness is doomed. A client who hides in her flat, refusing to allow friends and family to enter, apparently scorning all contact, is still relating to and communicating with those individuals. No matter how hard she tries to convince herself otherwise, she cannot escape the fact that they will receive and interpret a message from her actions and will seek to respond to it.

In his play *No Exit*, Satre (1944) famously describes the reality of the inherent relatedness of our existence in the phrase 'hell is other people'. And even those existential philosophers who see positive possibilities in our relatedness (Buber, for example) acknowledge that the unrelenting impact of others upon us and us upon others can be both rewarding *and* exhausting.

Clients who report finding it difficult to relate to others, or who find others frightening or even distasteful, and who struggle to manage the impact of their relationships with others on their wellbeing, can be invited by the existential therapist to explore their assumptions about relatedness. How would they describe their ways of relating to others? How do they experience the ways that others relate to them? Is it ever likely to be easy to live in a world with other people? Quite often such questioning leads the client to conclude that it is normal to find being-in-the-world-with-others to be a mixed blessing at best.

Heidegger (1978) terms the way we 'care' in relating to human beings in our world (as opposed to objects) 'solicitude'. It is useful to remember that our clients cannot overcome 'solicitude', as all human encounters demand our attention and matter to us in some way. And so our client mentioned above may feel delighted or horrified or any number of other emotions when her friends and family choose to respond by leaving her alone or by continuing to seek to interact with her, but she will not be oblivious to their actions. In some way or another, she will care.

8

THE UNIVERSALS OF HUMAN EXISTENCE

The universals of human existence are the conditions that pertain to every human life, across all cultures, and across all époques. These conditions are often referred to as 'givens', or the 'existentials' (Cohn, 2002).

Philosophers and practitioners focus their enquiries on different existential universals, making it difficult to establish a definitive list. However, almost all those that hold an existential perspective agree on these fundamental givens: freedom, temporality, facticity, which is also known as 'throwness' (Heidegger, 1972) (the specifics of our situation that are beyond our choice, e.g. the place of our birth, the fact of suffering and death), choice, death, uncertainty, isolation and relatedness, meaning and meaninglessness, guilt and anxiety. We could also include embodiment, sexuality, being-in-the-world, being-in-the-world-with-others and spatiality in this list.

Each and any of these givens have implications for the others; it is difficult to even speak of one aspect without referring to the others. For example, if we want to examine the given of *death* (something that existential practitioners influenced by Irvin Yalom's (1980) work might consider particularly significant), we would also be required to reference the factical dimension of birth, and how we have no control over either event. When a client discusses a difficult choice with us, we might find that their ability to choose is hampered by uncertainty in terms of securing a particular result or outcome, which in turn, could provoke anxiety.

These dimensions of human existence are inescapable: they affect everyone, all the time. Although at particular times in our clients' lives one concern may seem to be in the 'foreground', or the dominant aspect of their focus, in reality, all the other givens are in attendance.

What is valuable about the existential therapist's perspective on universals or givens is that they recognise that although these givens are inevitable, how any of us *respond* to these is a matter of choice. At the everyday level, for example, how one individual responds to the reality of their mortality (perhaps by exercising, eating healthily and rigorously protecting their skin from exposure to the sun) may be very different from how another client responds (by living according to the motto that 'life is too short', or by seeking everlasting life via religion).

Existential therapists do not impose a value judgement on such responses. Instead they provide a space where their clients can explore their reaction to the different universals and consider a full range of alternative stances. A client who reacts to his feelings of anxiety by imploring the therapist to cure him and make the feelings go away, for example, might find it beneficial to consider all the alternative ways they might respond to their anxiety: by accepting it, seeking medication to alleviate it, and so on. It is only through exploring these alternatives that the client will be able to come to terms with their responsibility to choose their response to each particular given.

9

THE ONTIC AND THE ONTOLOGICAL

Traditional philosophers have tended to concern themselves with seeking *facts* about *things*. Existential philosophers, however, make an important distinction between things or entities (describing them as ontic) and ideas or theories about things (describing them as ontological). Ontic refers to what is, and what can be observed and measured in some way. Ontological is about what it means to be – the theory or experience of a thing. So, for example, a doctor measuring a patient's anxiety through a psychological inventory is focusing on the ontic, while an existential philosopher seeking to understand the human given of anxiety is taking part in an ontological enquiry.

As human beings we are both ontic (we are entities that exist) and ontological (we are able to ask questions about our existence, to consider possibilities). We are the only beings that can do this – dogs, we can safely assume, do not wonder if there is more to life, nor do they lie awake at night pondering their own mortality.

The universals of human existence, such as mortality and isolation, are classed as 'ontological'. Something that is ontological is something we all share, a way in which we are all the same. The 'ontic' dimension of existence, on the other hand, is framed by our specific response to – and our unique engagement with – the ontological elements. Every ontological dimension has an ontic counterpart, i.e. a response, and every ontic element refers to an ontological aspect.

Our uniqueness as a human being is expressed in how we meet, or engage with, any of the givens of life. For example, as temporality is an element of life, *how* we as individuals relate to time, and the assumptions we hold about time, are ontic expressions of the ontological dimension of temporality.

Conversely, we can discern the ontological aspect(s) implied in any particular choice, behaviour or assumption. For example, a person who favours procrastination may be attempting to avoid or deny the ontological aspects of death and temporality by acting as if they have an endless amount of time available for their projects.

The existential counsellor will help their client to explore their ontic response to the ontological givens of existence. For example, work with a client who cries 'I just don't have time to get everything done' won't revolve around education in time management techniques. Instead the therapist will invite them to examine the particular ways in which they respond to the reality of having a finite amount of time and to consider how these responses serve or do not serve them.

10

EXISTENCE PRECEDES ESSENCE – CREATING A SELF OUT OF NOTHING

The essence of something consists of a predefined, typical set of characteristics that make it what it is. For example, the essence of a table is that it has legs and a flat surface and people put things on it (you may be able to think of other 'essential' characteristics). However, the existence of any one, individual, table may be different from this essence. It might have one, two, four or more legs, for example. It may have a broken leg or a bowed surface. It could be used for eating from, for working on or for placing things on. It might be made of wood or plastic or any number of other materials.

When Sartre coined the phrase 'existence precedes essence' he was reminding us that just as there are an infinite number of ways of being a table, there is no predetermined pattern, set of ideal characteristics or 'essence of human being', that we need to fit into.

The very word 'existence' is based on the Latin word 'existere', which means to 'stand out', or emerge (Macquarrie, 1972). The implication of this etymology is one of movement, transition and activity rather than solidity or fixedness. We could say that human beings stand out from nothingness, and from all other things and beings, and do so *continuously* by posing questions like 'How do I live?' and 'What shall I choose?'. It is these kinds of questions that indicate a quality of existence unique to us humans: we do not just *have* possibilities, we *are* possibilities. In this sense, we are differentiated from a rock, or other living things. Other living things do not appreciate the possibility of possibility.

For the existentialist, a human being is not a clearly defined object, or an essence that can be totalised, finalised or perfected. There is no 'human nature' that defines us. Therefore we cannot seek to understand another by slotting them into convenient typological boxes in the form of personality types, levels of intellect, groups of medical symptoms or astrological signs. In the therapeutic setting, these classifications serve only to hide the uniqueness of the individual by encouraging both parties to make assumptions about the client, thereby restricting that individual's awareness of her freedom to change.

We are not who we are because we are Capricorns, high on the introversion scale or members of Mensa. Rather, we become what we are by valuing some things over others, by choosing certain actions over others; and even then, we can 'repudiate' (Blackham, 1952/1978, p3), react to or revise this essence we have chosen.

When clients seek to categorise themselves – 'I am a depressive', 'I have my father's personality' – the existential therapist will be curious as to how and why they have chosen to identify these things as part of the 'essence' of who they are and what the implications of these choices are for that individual. More generally, they will encourage the client to explore the implications of seeing themselves as objects, with fixed, unchangeable ways of being in the world.

11

THE CONTRIBUTION OF PHENOMENOLOGY

Phenomenology as a philosophical movement has been practised in various guises for thousands of years, but grew in influence and popularity in the early twentieth century through the work of Husserl, Heidegger, Merleau-Ponty and Sartre. Husserl saw it as a rebuttal of the philosophical position taken by science to that point, and in particular its underlying assumption that human experience could and should only be measured through testing, quantifying and verifying hypotheses. He was intent on finding a method of investigating how things are experienced that would reveal their true nature, unfettered by assumptions and suppositions. He aimed to 'return to the thing itself' (Husserl, 1936, p34) through the application of the phenomenological method and hoped this method would ultimately become the basis of all scientific enquiry.

Husserl's transcendental form of phenomenology was criticised by Heidegger, among others, who argued that our experiences, ideas, values and perceptions are shaped by our interactions with the world in which we are immersed, making objective reality ultimately unknowable. Modern phenomenologists agree that reality is invariably subject to interpretation – as Spinelli (1989) proposes, we live in an interpreted world. Therefore the best we can hope for is to gain a better, more explicit knowledge and understanding of something through the phenomenological project.

Today's phenomenologists seek to capture lived experience – based on a paradigm of personal knowledge and subjectivity, and the importance of personal perspective and interpretation.

The focus is on our personal or shared meanings, as distinct from the objective physical world explored by science. The aim is to clarify the everyday, taken-for-granted human situations and events that we experience but typically do not notice, evaluate or question (Seamon, 2000). Rather than theorising about the stages of grief, for example, a phenomenologist would seek to understand the experience of grief through the eyes of those immersed in it.

For the existential therapist, phenomenology offers a powerful aid to understanding the subjective experiences of their clients and the potential to gain insights into their motivations and actions by 'cutting through the clutter of taken-for-granted assumptions and conventional wisdom' (Lester, 1999, p1). Clients are invited to describe their encounter with the world, to give voice to their experience, and be witnessed in doing so. This process often reveals hitherto unknown layers of meaning, generating surprising insights and new levels of understanding. As an approach, phenomenology offers the client the potential to make sense of their experience for themselves and ultimately to transform that experience (Finlay, 2011), should they choose to do so.

12

THE PHENOMENOLOGICAL METHOD

The Phenomenological Method is a research method designed to help us to clarify the interpretations we make and enable us to identify a clearer, less distorted description of how things are. Applied to a therapeutic setting, clients are encouraged to identify all the varied ways in which they attribute meaning to a particular aspect of their world.

The Phenomenological Method in existential therapy generally consists of three elements.

THE RULE OF EPOCHÉ

Epoché, a Greek word and one of the basic terms of stoic philosophy, means 'suspension of belief' (Cohn, 1997, p32). A psychotherapist practising this rule will attempt to 'bracket' their biases and assumptions with regard to what the client brings into the room. If we talk to a client before agreeing to see them, or if we receive referral notes, or even if we exchange emails briefly, we will have already begun to form our own theories about that client and the nature and origin of the issues they are facing. Existential counsellors seek a more flexible understanding and evaluation of what they perceive and try to set aside their assumptions, at least temporarily, in order to become more available to the unexpected aspects of the client and their story.

THE RULE OF DESCRIPTION

In this attitude, we are urged to examine things carefully, to describe, rather than explain. Explanation too often becomes the end of our enquiry into experience: we allow ourselves to rest in the finality of speculation and analysis. An existential practitioner will ask their clients to describe their immediate experience in ever-increasing detail and will gently resist presumed or posited explanations.

If the client can maintain a more generous stance towards their experience – working towards a faithful description of their 'immediate and concrete impressions' (Spinelli, 1989, p18) – then they may become more aware of the variables of their experience and the meanings and values they have ascribed to them, and of the alternative meanings they could apply.

THE RULE OF HORIZONTALISATION

Encouraging clients to look at and describe their story should precede any judgement as to what is more important. The therapist avoids placing a hierarchy on the importance of any of the elements of the client's description and treats all aspects of their report equally in terms of value, without regard to pre-ordained theories or assumptions. Again, this hopefully allows the client to develop a more expansive understanding of their experience.

Finally, the phenomenological paradigm indicates a distinction between experience as it occurs, known as 'straightforward' experience, and the interpretation of the experience or perception subsequently, which is known as 'reflective' experience (Spinelli, 2005). Reflective experience is part of the process of assigning meaning: it is at this point that we place evaluations on certain aspects of our straightforward experience, thereby relegating *some other* aspects to insignificance. This transpires because straightforward experience cannot be described in its entirety: it is impossible to reconstruct the lived reality in totality. As Husserl (2001, p168) states:

All three techniques are part of the phenomenological reduction – attempt to move away from the idea that consciousness and the world are two separate things (which is our natural attitude) – give us insight into the world as it is and go back to the things themselves.

13

INTENTIONALITY

As proposed previously, objects and entities *are*, but they do not *exist* in the way that human beings do. We, uniquely in our world, can engage with the things in our environment through our consciousness of them, and can ascribe meaning to them – we are meaning-construing beings.

Brentano examined this phenomenon and proposed that consciousness 'extends' itself towards objects and entities in the world: it (we) reaches out to the phenomena we meet, with the purpose of assigning meaning to them. This process is called 'intentionality', though it is not about the idea of doing something with a goal (or *intention*) but rather about the ability of our mind to form representations of people and objects in our world.

Husserl used the concept of intentionality to explain how we construct our reality. This 'reaching out' to the phenomena of the real world is regarded as an 'invariant relationship that exists between the real world and our conscious experience of it' (Spinelli, 2005, p12). In this way, the divide between consciousness and the world can be seen to be fictitious (Cohn, 1997). There are other beings and things in the world, but the act of intentionality makes them meaningful: they emerge, so to speak, through engagement with the human beings who construe them.

One of the givens of existence is *uncertainty*: we need to mitigate the anxiety provoked by uncertainty by assigning meaning to things; this is an attempt to understand them, to 'know' them in a way that takes the edge off the uncertainty of not-knowing. Not-knowing, not understanding the things around us would mean that we would be continually encountering them anew, having to appraise them afresh, being unsure of whether or not they represent a threat. People who go through traumatic experiences often find themselves questioning their appraisals of things they previously took for granted. For example, a client who survives a plane crash may suddenly find themselves frightened that the microwave might explode, or that a tree may fall on their head. Previously taken-for-granted conclusions about objects in the world are re-examined.

The opposite can also happen. The most certainty that we can ascribe to an object (or indeed a person) is its 'thing-ness'. By virtue of intentionality, we translate the phenomena around us, varied and chaotic as they are, into *things*; we then rest in the assurance that these things are stable, solid and predictable. Too often, however, clients become sedimented in their understanding of things, satisfied that they 'know' them totally and finally. They may say 'I know he won't ever change, he is just too stubborn', for example, or 'I'll never see the point in foreign films, they are so boring.'

The work of the existential therapist is to help the client to recognise that they cannot lay claim to a pure, static understanding of any phenomena, as what occurs is always an interpretation of the data that they perceive. In a highly creative fashion, we assign significance to phenomena, and in that sense we create their essence. But that essence can change. Sometimes it benefits a client to be open to new realities, to be willing to construct the meaning of particular entities anew. At other times the client needs to be supported in establishing a more solid sense of the essence of things in their world in order to reduce the anxiety produced by unusually high levels of uncertainty.

14

NOEMA AND NOESIS

Put simply, noema and noesis are the *what* and *how* aspects of the act of interpretation labelled intentionality. For every *what* there is, there is a *how* (an evaluation, an assignment of significance). For every instance of perception or awareness, there is an 'object' of awareness. If we experience, we experience *something*, and we experience it in *some way*, that is, with some meaning attached.

These focal points are readily distinguishable in theory, but in a lived situation we experience them simultaneously and, without conscious reflection, may not be able to separate them.

The meaning, value, or significance we attach to any experience will to some extent be shared by our social and cultural milieu. For example, most of us would recognise an object we commonly define as a 'hat'; however, *this* hat may hold specific significance or value for one person that is not shared by another.

Additionally, as we all hold a different perspective on the world, quite literally, the raw data, or the phenomena, which is available to one person, will not be available to another. For example, we may both have the same hat in our view, but I cannot see it from another person's perspective at the same time as they do. Even if I take up the view from their position, there are innumerable other variables, e.g. physical limitations like my eyesight or my height or the psychic variables like my mood or my level of attention, that will preclude the exact duplication of the experience of the hat.

So while our horizons may be shared by others, and our interpretation of what meets us there may overlap with that of our neighbour on occasion, ultimately each individual's perspective is unique. This has two significant implications for the existential therapist. First, it allows them to understand, at least partly, why communication with others can be so difficult. Helping clients to understand the unique nature of their experience is a key element of existential therapy. Second, it reminds the therapist never to assume that their understanding of what the client is saying is correct. They must approach even the most apparently straightforward statements made by the client with curiosity. For example, if a client rates his marriage as 9/10, the therapist could assume that this is realistically about as good as it could get, while the client might see this as a sign there are major failings in the relationship that need to be resolved. If therapists don't question their own assumptions, then a serious miscommunication is likely to take place.

15

RELATEDNESS AND THE FORMATION OF THE SELF

Our inter-connectedness with the world has significant implications for the concept of the self: the self and world are inextricably bound, therefore our concept of ourselves must be bound to the world as well.

Let's consider the terms 'self-concept' and 'self-construct'. For the existentialist, these expressions are particularly well named as they imply that our idea of our self is a creation or a fabrication.

In terms of phenomenology, we cannot have a perception of anything without some interpretative activity: this would, of course, include the experience we have of 'I'. And this interpretative activity is taking place all the time – we don't come up with one interpretation that we stick with, regardless of everything else that we experience afterwards. In the same way, our interpretation of who we are – our self-concept – isn't static either. We are not fixed entities in the scientific sense, then, but rather we are always in the process of becoming, of standing out or emerging (as Cooper (2003) reminds us, we are verb-like *happenings* rather than noun-like *things*).

So how does the person materialise or emerge? How does an 'I' move from nothing to something? The answer lies with other people. We exist relationally: we are in a world with others, and it is our engagement with the world and others that gives our 'self' a form. As we stand out from these elements, we distinguish our own-self from other selves, and from objects. Phenomenologically speaking, we make a comparison of 'I' with the 'not I' and from these perceptions we construct a meaningful concept of who 'I' is (Spinelli, 1989).

We are also a human subject: we bear more similarity to other people than to objects. This quality is a crucial aspect of our self-hood, because other people affect us, and serve to define us, in a manner that objects cannot.

Sartre tells the story of a man peering through a keyhole, and when he turns around and discovers that he too is being watched, he recognises that he is being judged and evaluated by the one who 'looks' at him.

It is in moments like these that we realise that other people have the power to define us: not totally, not finally, but certainly episodically. Other people can also change their opinion of us, for better or worse, and we thereby experience our self as mutable and impermanent. We exist as a 'self-in-relation' (Spinelli, 1994). It follows, therefore, that with every encounter with an Other, we may have our self-construct reinforced, or challenged; this can be experienced as a disturbing process, or can be welcomed as a creative dynamic.

We may each harbour ambitions to be experienced in some way or another: for example, I may wish to be perceived as kind, or intelligent; but the evidence for this aspiration must come from others, from the world, to be validated. I may attempt to lay claim to any valued characteristic, but if this claim is met with denial, I may well doubt my self-evaluation. Often the realisation that others define us in this way is difficult to accept and some clients may try to control the way other people see them, for example by being excessively concerned with the way they act, what they wear or how they look in front of others. Other clients may fret over what they perceive as erroneous or unjust views held by others as to who they (the client) actually are, expending a great deal of energy agonising over their inability to change the perceptions of 'the others'. An existential therapist will work with such clients to help them understand the universal nature of these judgements, encouraging them to consider the degree to which such assessments have, and should be, incorporated within their concept of themselves.

16

INTER SUBJECTIVITY

In the same way as other people mirror back to us a view of who they think we are, we also construct a view of others and communicate this back to them, through our words and actions. And the view we have of others doesn't reflect the 'truth' or 'reality', but rather emerges from who we are, from our experiences, values and beliefs.

> We don't see things as *they* are, we see things as *we* are.
> (Attributed to a variety of sources, including the Talmud)

This assertion aligns nicely with the existential phenomenological perspective. We experience others in the same way as objects: there is a *what* (or a *who*) and a *how*. The manner in which I experience them is subject to a variety of variables: cultural, social, political, personal, psychological, etc. A client who has grown up in a culture in which females are seen as home-makers, for example, may well perceive working mothers who employ nannies as bad mothers. Through existential therapy, this client can explore the fact that this is just an impression, and other ways of seeing the individual are possible and may or may not be of more benefit to the client.

The awareness that the constructs of self and other are not fixed or permanent can give rise to a great deal of anxiety: the other is not finally quantifiable, or knowable, and may therefore pose unknown risks to oneself or others.

Inter-subjectivity suggests that as we are always being-in-the-world-with-others, and as we are all invariably engaged in the intentional process, our self and other constructs are naturally fluid: however, we may cling stubbornly to our interpretations in an effort to make them permanent, so that we can rely on others, and the world, to behave in predictable ways.

17

FREEDOM, CHOICE AND RESPONSIBILITY

To begin our review of the concept of freedom, it might be useful to recall the ways in which human beings are *not* free: we cannot avoid or successfully evade the givens of existence – our freedom is always a situated freedom. Our freedom doesn't extend to all options: our options are limited by our existential situation, and the restrictions that are particular to any individual (their 'throwness'). At 5′ 3″ tall, I am not free to become an Olympic Gold medallist in the high jump, for example!

It is important that we recognise that we cannot and do not control many of the circumstances that we encounter; and it is not always readily apparent which circumstances we have had a hand in producing or to what extent. Our freedom is exercised in taking a stance to what meets us in life, even to that confusion about the possible contributions we make to our circumstances, whether benign or not. Existential therapy offers clients a space in which they can examine this freedom and identify circumstances in which they have more or less choice than they assumed. For example, both the client who states 'I can't stop myself from snapping at my partner all the time' and the client who is convinced that if they step on all the cracks on the pavement nothing bad will happen to their children, can fruitfully examine the boundaries of their freedom to choose.

We are always choosing, and the only choice we don't have is not to choose (even this is a choice in itself). Sartre acknowledges this when he states that 'we are condemned to be free' (Sartre, 1948/1973, p34). The fact that we have this freedom of choice, indeed we *must* exert this freedom and choose, provokes anxiety – we struggle to find a satisfactory basis for our choice, or a rational basis or a moral imperative or *some* principle that can ultimately guide us to make the 'right' choice. In choosing, we become aware of losing: if we make the wrong choice, we will be faced with a loss; if there are options, then one must be selected, and the others sacrificed, even if temporarily.

The anxiety connected to freedom and choice is a correlate of responsibility. As human existence is relational, our actions – our choices – have repercussions for others, and for our world; we are infinitely responsible, and our choices produce consequences that may have been beyond the scope of our understanding at the time we made them. It is this link between freedom and responsibility that led Victor Frankl (2004, p134) to declare:

> I recommend that the Statue of Liberty on the East Coast be supplemented by a Statue of Responsibility on the West Coast.

We can feel utterly alone in our responsibility: we can recognise that although it is *I* who chooses, it is *we* who bear the effects. It is for this reason that we attempt to assign responsibility for our choices to external sources, to our culture, to our upbringing, to fate.

18

THROWNESS, LIMITATIONS AND FINITUDE

'Throwness' (Heidegger, 1962) refers to the circumstances of human existence that are not chosen: birth, death, suffering, anxiety and the collection of other universal conditions, as well as those specifics of our situation, our culture, our particular physique, our family situation, etc. It is important to acknowledge that not only are these aspects that we have not chosen, neither can we control them; for example, we cannot always anticipate how or when we may incur suffering, we have no power over the exact timing or circumstances of our death (this is even true in cases of suicide), and we cannot undo the events of the past. We have some choice as to how we respond to these elements, indeed the choice of stance or attitude towards something may be the only choice we have, but the factical aspects cannot be nullified. Jaspers (1986) calls these aspects that can't be avoided or otherwise resolved 'limit-situations' and Macquarie (1972) outlines how our freedom is 'hedged in' by these situations.

It can be useful to recognise these limitations, both those that are ontological (the givens of existence), as well as those that are ontic (those that are specific to a person). However, our responses to the limitations are not primarily a matter of speculation: we discover ourselves in those instances in which we engage with them, and choose how to value them. A client who experiences many operations and painful medical procedures as a result of a congenital heart defect, for example, may choose to respond to their experience by becoming an expert in a dangerous sport such as hang-gliding, hence discovering in themselves an ability to manage and control fear and risk in a way that was not possible in response to their physical condition.

Kierkegaard (1844) used the term 'finitude' to describe the necessities we face in existence, and saw human existence as taking place between the necessities (finitude) and possibilities (the infinitude). The term finitude also alludes to the inevitability of change: we are witnesses to the imposition of change and transition. As I am here, now, occupying this space at this time, I cannot be elsewhere: my options are circumscribed. My perspective limits my possibilities: my position is unique, and ultimately unshareable. This is true for all others as well. The therapist can share the client's understanding of the core conditions of human existence but cannot hope to know exactly the client's response to those conditions, nor can they empathise fully with their client's situation. The client is to some extent always outside the understanding of the therapist, reinforcing the need for the client, and not the therapist, to retain the role of expert as far as their own life is concerned.

19

THE CENTRALITY OF ANXIETY, LOSS AND SUFFERING

Anxiety, in the existential perspective, is a given of existence: it differs from the affect or feeling of anxiety, and is sometimes referred to as 'anguish', 'angst' or 'existential anxiety'.

Both Heidegger and Sartre acknowledge Soren Kierkegaard as an important source for an understanding of this issue; his seminal work on the topic is translated into English as *The Concept of Dread* (Macquarrie, 1972).

Kierkegaard's particular contribution to the discussion is his description of anxiety as distinct from fear: fear has an object, we are afraid of something. Anxiety is a more generalised experience, without a specific focus; it is the hum in the background of all our activities, a presentiment of unknown origins and unforeseeable consequences.

Kierkegaard proposes further that anxiety is connected to freedom. Freedom puts us in contact with possibilities, and the risks involved in committing to any particular action or choice. As we stand on the precipice of choice, we are faced with a 'dizziness of freedom' (Kierkegaard, 1844, p61). Possibilities appear in the negative sense as well: it is possible that things may not turn out as we expected; in fact, our choices can precipitate loss and tragedy for ourselves and others. There is much to lose: our hopes, our desires, the future as we anticipated it would be. There is a distinct possibility, in fact inevitability, that if you chose, you lose. With the choice of any one option, other options are lost to us. Paradoxically, then, the more that we choose, the more anxious we may feel. Sometimes we may respond to this reality by attempting to get others to choose for us – a client may try to manipulate their partner into ending their relationship by behaving unreasonably, for example, in order to avoid the anxiety of making a choice they may later regard as 'wrong'. Similarly, our clients may try to get us, the therapist, to choose for them, again, as an attempt to avoid the anxiety that comes from taking responsibility for their own choices.

Anxiety is treated similarly by Heidegger, who echoes the proposal that anxiety has no definite object; it is about being-in-the-world in general. Heidegger relates anxiety to death, chance and nothingness. He also points out the anxiety that comes from realising that everything we consider intrinsically meaningful in our lives, all the things that we think of as 'givens' – the way we bring up our children, the way we think and act, the way we relate to other people – are in the end but social constructions and could all be otherwise (Cooper, 2003). Clients who bring a sense of meaninglessness to the therapeutic endeavour may well have become aware at some level of the way in which we play roles in a world empty of intrinsic meaning. The challenge is to engage them in the daily search for personal meaning that will allow them to re-connect with their world.

There is some agreement among these authors as to the positive effect of anxiety: it can awaken us to the way we are engaging with the world, and we can choose to engage differently. The anxious client can be encouraged to hear what the anxiety is telling them about the way in which they engage with the world and how they might choose to engage differently. They can consider the notion that anxiety is normal and inevitable and that freedom is a blessing and a burden; any attempt to evade this demand, and bury our head in busy-ness, only results in more anxiety.

20

DEATH AND NOTHINGNESS

Sartre (1948/1973, p26) declared that human beings have no solidity, no 'core' or determined characteristics in terms of selfhood. When we stand on the threshold of a choice, it may be at that juncture that we realise that there is nothing *inside* ourselves that ultimately provides a satisfactory guide to making an imminent choice the 'right' choice (particularly when it is a difficult choice). We may also appreciate that in making a choice, we *make* ourselves, for we are attempting to affect the world, the future, and to establish who and how we are.

This nothingness, this emptiness inside, is what we seek to address, to fill up, with our actions, beliefs and assumptions – which collectively we can describe as our 'worldview'. Sometimes we are successful in filling this void with an enduring worldview, only to find the meanings and values we ascribe to are suddenly, often catastrophically, challenged by an event or change in circumstances that leads us to question much or all of what we hold dear. This can result in us feeling that nothing makes sense anymore, that everything is pointless and without meaning. At this point we may seek therapeutic help to deal with something that in every day terms is described as a nervous breakdown, but would be seen by existential thinkers as an 'existential crisis'.

When we recognise, probably at a very early age, that we and those around us will die, that we will cease to be, this possibility of non-being dramatically provokes a sense of contingency: everything could be otherwise; *I* could be otherwise. In recognising that everything could be non-existent, it is a short step to realise that *I* too could be non-existent. Such an appreciation of contingency can engender a sense of futility: what I do, think, feel, or become has no intrinsic meaning; the value I choose to ascribe to anything is based on nothing._

Death is probably the most difficult dimension of existence to acknowledge and engage with – indeed Yalom (1980) believes that a failure to confront our own mortality is at the root of many psychological symptoms and conditions. A common misperception about existentialism is that it is all about death. In fact it is less about death itself and more about how we deal with the realisation that death is something that will happen to us. Existential therapy helps the client to define how they want to live in the shadow of this reality. Heidegger (1962) proposes that although death is the end of all possibilities – it is the final defining eventuality, and makes us 'beings-towards-death' – it is also the eventuality that 'saves' us (Heidegger, 1962). When we acknowledge, at the deepest level, that we are mortal, and that we must make our choices in light of this eventuality, we may awake to a different perspective on our activities.

To recognise death as an end to all of our projects is to see it as a boundary: it creates an outline to the experience of life, in much the same way as birth does. Facing up to our death can engender a sense of extreme isolation: it is the eventuality that no one can share, no one can stand in my place. The anxiety provoked by such a realisation can prompt us to flee into denial and evasions (a state Heidegger describes as 'fallen'). A client who spends his fortune investigating ways to delay or avoid death may be encouraged to evaluate the costs and benefits of his way of dealing with the existential given of death. He may realise that in seeking to postpone death, he is actually postponing life. De Beauvoir (1948, p120) sums this stance up perfectly when she states:

> Today, however, we are having a hard time living because we are so bent on outwitting death.

If, on the other hand, he commits to living with the possibility of his own death at the forefront of his mind, using it to guide his decisions about how to live life in line with what he most values, then he rises to the challenge that death poses.

21

EXISTENTIAL GUILT

Existential guilt, like existential anxiety, is not an affect; it is instead an inevitable, ineluctable dimension of human existence.

Everyday guilt is what we experience when we are aware of having broken the rules or been in the wrong in some way. Boss (1979) distinguishes between this and neurotic guilt (excessive preoccupation with something that isn't deserving of condemnation but which our parents might not approve of) and existential guilt that comes from not having taken action when we ought to have. Heidegger argues that we have primordial guilt, because we are always in the world in a state of incompleteness – there is always something more we could achieve or complete. Existential guilt is a consequence, therefore, of the human being existing as possibility. As there is no essence to the human being, one is free to realise possibilities that are available, or one may fail to do so. As we always 'lag behind' (Cohn, 1997) our possibilities, our failure to realise them provokes existential guilt.

The existential therapist will see existential guilt as a sense of unease that, like anxiety, has something to tell the client about their values and the ways in which they are, or are not, living their life in line with those values. Clients may try to evade or avoid acknowledging their freedom, the possibilities in their lives, and the inescapable necessity of choice, getting caught up in 'everydayness' (ending up in the state Heidegger (1978) describes as 'fallen'). Clients in this state often appear totally preoccupied with the minutiae of their lives, and the lives of those around them, and avoid any discussion that risks exposing or holding up to examination the core beliefs and values that make up their worldview.

Existential anxiety and existential guilt are closely associated: when we experience existential anxiety, it can engender an awareness that we must choose; if we 'refuse' to choose, which is also a choice, we may then experience the indebtedness, the guilt that ensues when we struggle to avoid this given.

In acknowledging the guilt, however, we rediscover the possibilities open to us – we experience what Heidegger (1978) describes as 'the call of conscience' – a moment of insight in which we see ourselves as clearly responsible for our own decisions, and actions, and for acknowledging our guilt and indebtedness to *being* itself. In this moment we can reach towards our potentialities and choose for ourselves. Existential guilt in these circumstances is a 'mentor on the path towards greater freedom' (Cooper, 2003, p26).

22

AUTHENTICITY AND INAUTHENTICITY, BAD FAITH AND GOOD FAITH

Authenticity is a concept that is much debated in existential circles and is not to be confused with being genuine, in the everyday sense. To understand it, we can refer back to the fact that we often try to avoid the despair or unease of existential anxiety or existential guilt by turning a blind eye to the realities of our existence, including the fact that we are constantly in a state of becoming. A client may state that they are a 'fitness fanatic' and therefore never miss a day at the gym, or they may bemoan the size of their waistline, claiming that they are just not good at exercising. Either way they exist inauthentically by denying the freedom of choice they have and inferring that they are fixed and unchanging objects.

Sartre calls this being in 'bad faith'. Put simply, bad faith is a pretence that that we are not as free as we actually are, *or* that we are more free than we actually are. Sartre (1948/1973) asserts that in order to avoid the anxiety attached to choosing, and having to choose on the basis of values that are based on oneself, which is essentially *nothing*, we attempt to recreate ourselves as an object, a thing, an essence. If we have an essence or core self, then we are determined by that Self, and our choices are limited, if not totally pre-determined.

If we define ourselves by our roles, our activities, our place in society, in fact in any way at all, we are practising bad faith. The same is true when we try to objectify others: to make them predictable, solid, knowable in the way that objects seemingly are knowable. Such objectification often results in relationship crises as each partner seeks to objectify the other as 'in the wrong', 'unreasonable', 'untidy', etc., while fiercely resisting their partner's attempts to categorise them in similar ways. An existential therapist will work with the parties in the relationship to explore the ways each objectifies the other and to open the door to alternative possibilities by asking questions like 'is this always true of your partner?' and 'can you think of times when you didn't behave in this way?'.

Conversely, some clients are in bad faith because they behave as though they have all possibilities open to them, without factical constraints like their history, their situation, the needs of the other and all the attending existential limitations. Such individuals may find it difficult to accept the constraints imposed by the other's needs and expectations. The therapist's role in this scenario is to remind the individual of the need to embrace their freedom to choose to remain in the relationship or not, rather than hide behind the inauthentic stance that they are trapped by it.

Authentic existence is a way of being-in-the-world, as is inauthentic existence. Authenticity and inauthenticity are *both* unavoidable aspects of existence and neither is essentially 'good' or 'bad'. Indeed, inauthenticity is arguably the more primary, pervasive condition (Deurzen & Kenward, 2005). It is inevitable that we will lose ourselves in the everyday world and become lost in 'the crowd'. However, it must be noted that authentic existence is *not* a retreat from the world, or from being-with-others. Rather, it is about creating our own values and rejecting the stock morality of the group (Warnock, 1970).

Authenticity is also not about saying exactly what we think or feel at any particular moment. Rather, it is about acting in line with our values, living every day in the knowledge that nothing 'just is' and everything is fragile and contingent.

An existential therapist aids her clients in the active examination of the 'givens' in their life. Clients who make objectifying statements like 'it's weak to cry' or 'I don't have any choice' or 'it's just the way life is' are gently invited to explore the reality of these accounts, to confront the consequences of having become alienated from what is important to them. If they can openly acknowledge the boundaries of existence (including freedom, choice, responsibility, anxiety and death), if they are willing to 'stand naked in the storm of life' (Becker, 1973, p86), then they are adopting a more authentic stance.

The possible benefit of an authentic engagement with life is the realisation of our power to value things as one sees fit, even if these evaluations are subject to impermanence. An authentic attitude frees us to choose freely.

23

MEANING AND ABSURDITY IN A MEANINGLESS COSMOS

In every perception, we evaluate what we perceive: to even describe an object is to value it in some way. This is a description of how meaning and value are construed in our relational world. Every time we encounter someone or something we interpret it and our understanding of it changes, or shifts in focus (Spinelli, 2007), creating a new understanding: our interpretations of ourselves, our world and the objects and people in it therefore are infinitely variable; indeed, one might say they become meaningless.

It may seem absurd, indeed futile, for a being construed of 'nothing' to attempt to assign meaning to the world, and to others. What is the source of our evaluations, if they are so contingent, based as they are on circumstances that could all be otherwise? How bizarre it may seem that the evaluator, who attributes essences, has no essence of his/her own?

The absurdity of existence, of being, is revealed in the question posed by Heidegger (1978): 'Why is there something rather than nothing?'. There is no answer forthcoming: it is absurd.

And yet many existential thinkers believe that a human being's most basic drive is to find meaning. Indeed, one kind of existential therapy – Logotherapy (Logis being the Greek term for 'meaning') – is based on the premise that psychological unease, emptiness and despair can be overcome if an individual can identify the meaning in their existence. As Frankl (2004, p97) states:

> He who has a *why* to live can bear with almost any *how*.

In much the same way that humans have no essence, life, it is said, has no inherent meaning. If someone holds a religious belief that provides meaning(s), we can also appreciate that the believer has chosen this source; in fact, faith has little currency if it is not accompanied by doubt and choice.

However, it would seem that to stand in the heat of meaninglessness, which would also imply chaos, is an intolerable state. To even begin to evaluate one option over another, we need to formulate a plan, a route that aims at a hoped-for future. Fortunately, it is a function of freedom that it allows, in fact demands, that we create values: we can choose how to live, which principles to abide by, what meaning to ascribe to our lives.

These meanings and ethical values must be freely chosen in order to place us in an authentic engagement with those values: a subscription to any dogma is an article of bad faith. Sartre proclaims through the character of Orestes: 'Every man must find his own way' (Sartre, 1955, p121–122).

In existential therapy, clients are challenged to be explicit about the meaning they accord to their lives and to explore alternative meanings, shedding light on alternative ways of being in the world. Where there is a sense of meaninglessness, clients are encouraged to explore what is important to them, how they could respond to their circumstances and how they might understand their actions, in order that they might find their own unique *why* to live for. As Frankl (2004, p117) explains:

> The person without meaning is like a mountain climber who enters a dense fog and, lacking the goal before his eyes, is in danger of succumbing to a total weariness.

24

TEMPORALITY AND ORIENTATION TOWARDS THE FUTURE

The nature of time is something that has long been the subject of philosophy. Aristotle (384–322 BC) linked time to change and movement; Husserl argued that time is lived experience; and Heidegger proposed that the basis for an understanding of the existence of human beings is that of time. Cohn (2002, p62) reflected on this when he stated:

> It might be said that human beings don't just live in time, but in fact they 'live time'.

'Temporality' is a term that usually refers to how we experience time, rather than time as it is measured. It is the experience of time, the significance of time, that interests philosophers. Existential philosophers see the 'objective' measurement of time, where it is imagined to be linear, with an endless series of present moments, as inauthentic: 'Time is not an entity but a human activity' (Deurzen & Kenward, 2005, p202).

In speaking of measured time, we refer to the past, the present and the future. All three of these designations are cross-referential: it is difficult to even construct a sentence without alluding to some aspect of time, but in so doing we implicitly or explicitly refer to all three of these categories. Sartre talked about the past as *being in-itself*, by which he meant it is fixed and has no possibilities, and the present as *being-for-itself*, as being free and full of possibilities. With reference to this, existential thought posits that we are our possibilities, and that these possibilities draw us towards the future; the future holds the end of all possibilities in terms of our death. It might be said, therefore, that it is the future that has a greater bearing on us than the past or the present: we deliberate and review in an effort to make the decision that creates the future we hope for. This has implications for our capacity to be content or satisfied with our lives – unlike the acorn, that is unaware of the possibility of becoming an oak tree, we human beings always live in the shadow of our possibilities, aware that we could be better, more or different than we are now. In these circumstances, existential therapists recognise the quest for contentment or happiness as doomed to failure.

The concept of facticity relates to our history, for example, where we were born, into what family, what culture, with what particular physiology, as well as the givens of existence proposed earlier. These factical elements can place limitations on our options, but we are free to assign value and meaning to these considerations. In this sense, existential therapy can be a place where clients change their past through assigning it different meaning or significance in the present and therefore changing the impact it will have on their future.

The dimension of existence that we call the 'present' is also *informed* by our anticipation of the future. The 'present' is experienced, but can only be described and made meaningful in retrospect: the moment itself escapes us. The value of existential therapy, indeed of any therapy, is that it provides a place in which we can stand outside of ourselves and experience the 'moment of vision' (Heidegger, 1978) – where we can oversee the past, present and future as it exists for us as an individual.

Time is one of the boundaries of existence. To the extent that we allow ourselves to be aware of these concerns, we are living authentically. If we harbour a longstanding imbalance in the focus on any one of the temporal categories, we can create our own limits to authentic living. A client who is obsessive over aspects of their past may need help to consider their experiences and clarify the extent to which they want to be defined by them going forward. If a focus on the future means the client is living a life devoid of meaning in the present, they may find it useful to examine the gains and losses in a strategy that takes for granted a future they may not have. The key is to understand that we can own our past, present and future rather than feeling it is imposed upon us (Deurzen & Adams, 2010).

25

EMBODIMENT AND THE WORLD

Many existential philosophers emphasise the fact that the body is more than a vehicle for the mind. Merleau-Ponty (1962) in particular emphasises the fact that we both *have* a body, and *are* a body, that is we are inextricably bodily beings (Cooper, 2003). We experience and participate in and indeed understand the world through our body, by touching, seeing, thinking and communicating. Perception is only possible through the body.

Being-in-the-world is always conceived as a psychosomatic unity; the division of mind and body most famously proposed by Descartes (1596–1650) may be useful in intellectual debate, but our experience is of unification. It may be that one or the other of these aspects has our attention, but further reflection will reveal that both aspects must be present for a human being.

My body gives me a point of view on the world, and the means of participating in the world; my body also provides the place for others to have a view on me, and interact with me. My bodily experiences are often the most direct means I have of understanding the world and it's impact on me and indeed may tell me as much about my way of being as intellectual reflections. As Nietzsche (1967) writes:

> There is more wisdom in the body than in thy deepest learnings.

Embodiment has particular relevance for inter-subjectivity. The other can hold a viewpoint on me that I can never have on myself: they can 'see' me from a perspective that will always escape me. I, too, have the same advantage over the other. In moments when I experience shame, or pride, it is in that instance that I am some*thing* for the other, and I am alienated from myself, as I experience my body 'not as it is for me but as it is for the other' (Macquarrie, 1972, p115).

Existential therapy assumes that the client is physically attuned to the world and considers aspects of the client's physical world as equally significant to other aspects of their experience. Subjects for therapeutic enquiry might include the messages the client's body and body image portray to the world; the extent to which, and the different ways, the client uses their body to communicate; the client's ease or lack of ease with their physical self; the way in which the client chooses to strengthen or build upon the insights offered by their physical existence; how the client experiences others as they engage with her embodied self, and so on. In these and other ways our bodies give us vital access to the truth of our being (Guignon, 2002). In recognising this, existential therapy helps the client to engage fully in living by experiencing it deeply and concretely rather than just having theories about it (Deurzen & Adams, 2010).

26

AN EXISTENTIAL PERSPECTIVE ON SEXUALITY

Sexuality is not limited to a particular act: it is not entirely physical, emotional nor psychological. It is a potential: it can be deployed in physical activity that might be deemed sexual, or it can be actualised when one is alone, as a flight from relatedness. If solo expression of sexuality as a rejection of relatedness becomes the dominant form in which sexuality is expressed, it can become a futile and problematic pursuit, as in obsessive use of pornography, for example.

Sexuality is an aspect of embodiment: as humans, we are a unity of consciousness and physicality. Our bodies are what 'keeps the visible spectacle constantly alive' (Merleau-Ponty, 1962, p203). The body makes it possible for us to be with others: it is via our embodiment that we exist for and with others, although it is not the only way we participate with others.

Smith-Pickard and Swynnerton, in Deurzen and Arnold-Baker (2005, p50), expand the notion of sexuality beyond the definitions of activities that refer primarily to preferences for partners or behaviours. In contrast to the usual understanding of sexuality in this regard, they propose that:

> Sexuality thus becomes reified as a defining characteristic of an individual rather than remaining at the level of description of a fundamental aspect of intersubjectivity, as it would be seen from an existential perspective.

In his review of the philosophical proposals of Sartre, Merleau-Ponty and Berdyaev, Macquarrie (1972, p116) summarises: 'human sexuality is not just a biological function but has its inescapable ontological dimension'. The dimension referred to here is inter-subjectivity: this is the realm in which our expectations, aspirations and assumptions about ourselves and others are manifest in our worldview, and actualised in our choices and behaviours. Even those activities that would be described as auto-eroticism would have repercussions for the social contexts of any given individual.

The client that comes to therapy is primarily concerned with the ontic manifestations of this philosophical understanding of sexuality: they wish to address a problem specific to their way of being sexual. This may be with respect to sexual orientation, attitudes relevant to sex or sexuality, or sexual performance.

For the existential practitioner, their understanding of these concerns will be grounded in an appreciation of the universal aspects of existence that might be implicated in these dilemmas: as discussed, certainly relatedness, finitude, temporality, responsibility, freedom, choice, anxiety, uncertainty, guilt and suffering are all concerns that can play a part in the formulation of any specific dilemma. These issues in themselves are not necessarily problematic: it is the client's manner of our engagement with them that can give rise to discomfort and distress.

The existential therapist will invite the client to explore the meanings of their experiences in order to gain, along with the client, a more expansive understanding of their worldview as it is implicated in this difficulty. Where acceptance on the part of the therapist generates trust, the client will be more willing to discover and reflect on their own vulnerabilities, and on the ambiguities and partial truths of their perspectives.

The worldview is expansive, mostly implicit, and mutable; what may seem like diversions are more likely to be aspects that are implicitly relevant to the situation under discussion. No avenue of exploration is deemed irrelevant; to stay with the client in this endeavour takes diligence, and a deep respect for the client's perspective, in spite of our own assumptions and values. This can be particularly challenging in an area where desires and practices are so readily characterised as 'normal' or 'deviant' within the wider culture in which the therapy takes place.

27

CONSCIOUSNESS AND THE UNCONSCIOUS

To be conscious is to be aware, and to be aware is always to be aware of something. To be conscious and aware doesn't mean that we retain all that we encounter: it would be impossible to take in all the raw stimuli that come our way and hold them in our awareness. For the existentialist, although they might accept the fact that not all mental phenomena are conscious – this doesn't mean that we have a separate or distinct unconscious mind in the sense that Freud (2013) envisaged.

When we perceive, we are able to distinguish one thing from another due to our ability to focus on one item as it *stands out* from another; if we could not perceive this differentiation, everything would be an unintelligible blur (Spinelli, 1989, 1994). This ability to discern boundaries creates a figure/ground configuration: the article that occupies the focus of our attention is foreground, that is, more prominent, and the other phenomena are relegated to the background. The articles that are not attended to do *not* disappear from our perception, at least not until we shift our attention or change our perspective; the data remain.

It is noteworthy that this process is inter-relational: by comparing the qualities or characteristics of one phenomenon with those of another the distinction becomes clearer. This holds true for intra-psychic objects, like emotional states, e.g. sad as opposed to happy, or characterisations of self and other, e.g. I am more generous than someone who is miserly.

The things we are aware of, that become the foreground and background of our perception, are those that hold some interest or value for us at that juncture; the significance could be positive, as something that makes one happy, or less desirable, as something that might be dangerous. All other data becomes irrelevant (Cohn, 1997).

Additionally, we can 'dissociate' perceptions and experiences that are unacceptable or unpleasant; in this case we re-direct or withdraw our awareness from our experience. This might be termed 'denial': we disavow the significance the experience has for us.

However, these perceptions remain conscious: they are assigned a place in the distant background of the figure/ground configuration, until such a time as they are brought 'forward' for more attentive deliberation.

Examples of this dynamic abound: most of us will have made a comment to the effect of 'I didn't believe I was capable of doing/thinking/believing such a thing'. In this situation we become aware in an experiential sense of what we already 'knew'. The denied experience is apprehended in its renewed signification; one might say it is 'allowed'.

Existential therapy focuses not only on the foreground but also on the beliefs, thoughts, feelings and perceptions that make up the background to our experiences. We can liken this activity to the exploration of a dark attic room, where clients are asked to shine their torches not only on the items closest to them or on one particular side of the room, but also on those items partially obscured by other things or stored in the far corners of the room. In existential terms, this room is entirely open to analysis and the idea of *the* unconscious as a *place* where provocative or repugnant experiences are stored and guarded by a 'censor' is redundant. Cannon (1991, p38) summarises a position ascribed to Sartre, but one that resonates with most existential thinkers:

> Consciousness is … an openness towards Being, a desire or lack of a future fullness rather than a self-contained, intra-psychic system.

The things that we are conscious of can, of course, be distorted or blurred by self-deception (or bad faith), but by drawing attention to these and other aspects of our experience relegated to the less-illuminated parts of our mind, they can be reviewed, reflected upon and assigned a new meaning.

28

ABSOLUTE TRUTH, THE NOT-KNOWING AND THE UN-KNOWING

Knowing comes from consciousness, and consciousness is always consciousness of something (intentionality). That something is only given meaning because of our throwness and our existing experience with the world. There is therefore no such thing as 'a truth', only 'truths' as people perceive them. Human beings are 'thrown' into the world: that is, the particulars of their entrance into the world, and the givens of existence, including having a past, all serve to situate them in a unique perspective; each person's horizon is particular to that person. Therefore, our vision of truth, which is an evaluation of one's experience, is limited. The notion of an absolute or final truth that exists independently of a human perspective is not credible.

Furthermore, we are always on our way: moving towards a future that is potential and eventual; this movement, too, will affect how we value our perception, and how we qualify our experience.

Often clients come to therapy seeking the comfort they anticipate would come from knowing things finally and certainly; they want to be better able to predict the effects of their decisions, to be relieved of the anxiety of uncertainty and the burden of responsibility. If this certainty were possible, however, if we could *know*, we would not be free; we would be the *massif* of Sartre's description, a solid object without possibility or consciousness.

Existential therapy seeks to enquire into the client's experience by asking them to suspend what they think they know, by joining in a journey with the client in which they become, temporarily at least, unknowing, open to novelty, surprise and wonder (Deurzen & Adams, 2010). Everything is open to debate and the client learns to tolerate doubt and self-doubt and to resist the temptation to prematurely conclude their investigations in the hope that what they discover will be of value to them and their journey.

Such conscious reflection can allow them to re-construct their experience, and how they interpret it: the phenomena may be more adequately revealed in its complexities, which in turn can allow the client a different understanding. This stance of un-knowing, or naïveté, permits a wider range of possibilities.

29

A THEORY OF EMOTIONS

Heidegger (1962) states that we are always related to the world in a certain 'tone', by which he means that we are always in a state of mind or in a mood. Moods are *disclosive* – they alert us as to how we find ourselves in the world. A mood, feeling or emotion is a response to what we encounter, and also reveals what we encounter. We participate in the world via moods: there is a sense of 'attunement', to use Heidegger's term.

Emotional responses are always concomitant with cognitive and physiological responses: this reflects a totality of how human beings are in the world.

As we are always 'attuned' to how we are in the world, it follows that we are always in some kind of emotional experience. Additionally, as we can have our own experience as a focus of reflection, we can have emotions *about* emotions. For example, I may be angry with my colleague, and I can also feel guilty about being angry. It follows from this proposal that more than one emotion is present at any given time; one emotion may be in the foreground, and others in the background.

As our being-in-the-world is a dynamic of 'standing out', our attunement is active as well; consequently, our emotional experience is in flux. The figure/ground configuration is also a mobile model: elements of foreground and background move and exchange positions.

Emotions, like any experience, are one of two foci of 'intentionality', the invariant of perception. As a response to what we meet in the world, including intra-psychic phenomena, there is a *what* that invokes a *how*: we are therefore emotional *about* something. What we are emotional about will be something that holds some kind of value and significance for us: emotions reveal what matters to us, and how they matter to us.

For Sartre, emotions also act as an escape from our predicaments. When a client dwells on the loss of their job and the sadness they feel about this event, they may avoid the difficult realities that unemployment brings. If I am consumed by jealousy each time my partner suggests that they spend a weekend away alone, I avoid facing the terror of abandonment; if I vomit with disgust every time my child cuts their knee, I avoid dealing with the reality that I cannot protect them from pain.

Feelings, moods and emotions are not distortions of 'reality', however: they are involvement with what meets us, albeit involvement that may distort our true engagement with something, as the examples above show. Polt (1999, p66) gives the example of fear: it does not remove us from something; it 'reveals' something as threatening.

An existential therapist maintains a stance of openness and curiosity towards their client's emotional world, helping them to identify what their emotions reveal about their view/ experience of the world, recognising those emotions that they are not aware of and encouraging them to accept the simultaneous experience of two or more apparently contradictory emotions. This enables them to experience the full spectrum of emotions in all their vibrancy and passion, for as Bugental (1987, p126) points out:

> Emotionality is a unitary dimension of being: one suppresses one aspect at the cost of crippling all.

30

THE FOUR WORLDS: PHYSICAL, PERSONAL, SOCIAL, SPIRITUAL

Ludwig Binswanger was a Swiss psychiatrist who trained as a psychoanalyst under Jung but later became interested in the work of existential writers, most notably Husserl, Buber and Heidegger. He developed a structure for understanding and exploring a person's worldview based on three dimensions of existence – the Umwelt or physical world, the Mitwelt or social/public world and the Eigenwelt or psychological/personal world. This model was adapted by Deurzen (1997), and a fourth dimension – the Überwelt or spiritual world – was added to the original three.

Many existential therapists use this model as a basis for thinking about and exploring their clients' worldviews. Deurzen-Smith (1995, p9) suggests that when clients describe their experience of each of the worlds in detail they gain insights into how they see the world and their place within it and 'become truthful with themselves again'.

The *Umwelt or physical dimension* refers to embodiment and the physical environment. This is the most fundamental of the dimensions, as we cannot be human without having a physical presence, and without being affected by the elements in our environment, be they humanly constructed or natural forces. Many of the physical aspects of our world are givens, and our response to these limitations is what is of therapeutic interest. Key polarities within this dimension include birth versus death and expansion versus contraction of the physical world.

The *Mitwelt or social/public dimension* comprises everyday social interactions; this would include our attitudes towards public constructs such as race, gender, class or family, for example. It would also include ways in which we relate to others, and contains polarities such as trust versus distrust, competition versus cooperation and conformity versus individualisation. This dimension reflects the premise that we are always being-in-the-world-with-others.

The *Eigenwelt or personal/private dimension* is that which reflects our attitudes and assumptions about the intimate others in our lives, as well as the view that we hold of ourselves. This is the dimension we most commonly associate with counselling, as it involves the person's relationship to his or her self and to family, close friends, etc. (Deurzen & Kenwood, 2005). In this context we may discern how the client values, or devalues, themselves, as well as the meaning and attitudes they hold with reference to their closest friends and family. Polarities in this dimension include self-acceptance versus self-development and authenticity versus inauthenticity.

The fourth dimension is the *Überwelt or spiritual dimension*, which includes our assumptions and perspectives on the world, the universe and the cosmos. Here we find our philosophical and spiritual values and assumptions about life, and the sphere beyond. This is something of a meta-context, which references all the other perspectives attributed to the other three dimensions. Polarities within this world include meaning versus meaninglessness, good versus evil and transcendence versus mundanity.

These dimensions are inter-connected and cross-referential, in much the same way as the givens of existence: it is difficult to consider one without implicating the others.

This model is a structure by which we can begin to understand our own and others' worldview. It helps the therapist to stand back from the client's day-to-day concerns and ensure that all the different aspects of their reality are explored (Cooper, 2003). Where there is an emphasis on one dimension in a person's concerns, or when there is a paucity of reference to any particular category, these imbalances are suitable focal points for reflection and exploration.

31

WORLDING, WORLDVIEW, VALUES AND SEDIMENTED BELIEFS

We are constantly interacting with the world, interpreting it on the basis of these interactions and adding these perceptions to a self-concept that is in permanent flux.

The dynamism of our existence isn't reflected in phrase fragments like 'worldview' or 'figure/ground', or even 'being-in-the-world'. The term 'worlding' has been adopted by Spinelli (2007) to restore a sense of movement, and openness to the concepts that form the basis for understanding existence from an existential phenomenological viewpoint. Worlding is the lived process of existing: it is dynamic, and it is indescribable in that it can never be pinned down and fully appreciated in its 'now-ness': it can be taken as an object, dismantled, and reflected upon only subsequently. In so doing, we get something like a 'snapshot' of the living existent; it cannot be a complete representation of experience in time.

The idea of worlding is often a useful one for clients who impose rigid self-constructs upon themselves or others, as it encourages them to see themselves as more malleable and less stuck than they might otherwise have done. Of course, this flexibility can also herald the anxiety that comes from recognition of our freedom, which may make this insight something of a double-edged sword.

The worldview is quite simply made up of our assumptions, attitudes and values about oneself, others, the world and the cosmos. These categories closely reflect those set out by Deurzen (1997) in the four-worlds model. The worldview will reflect those concerns deemed ontological, as described previously; however, these universal aspects will be manifest ontically, that is, they will be demonstrated in the particular ways that we each engage with these aspects. For example, one universal given is that of anxiety. While one client may engage with anxiety by seeking anti-anxiety medication, another might take to drink or drugs and yet another may accept that anxiety, though unpleasant, is normal and something that can provide helpful insights into their choices

Values are an important constituent of our worldview and elucidation of them in a therapeutic setting can be illuminating. If a client holds a value that money is the most important objective in life, then how do their aspirations and goals reflect or mitigate against this? What implications does this value have for how they wish to be experienced, and how they choose their friends? In what ways does this value also influence how the client creates his physical environment, and how he conducts himself with reference to social etiquette.

It is the values and assumptions that support our worldview that inform behaviour. However, it can be readily observed that the worldview can harbour contradictions, inconsistencies and paradoxes that may remain obscured: these elements become apparent when they are experienced as ineffective strategies for dealing with life. It is often in the description and review of those contradictions that the most insight is gained.

There are instances when our assumptions may be challenged. I assume that when I cross the street when the crossing shows a green light that traffic coming from the other direction will stop for me, because others will respect the law as I do. However, there have been occasions when this was not the case. At those junctures, I may review my assumption for its validity or effectiveness. If I can allow the unexpected experience to inform my assumption, I may construct a new assumption that integrates the novel possibilities I have encountered. If these new insights are incorporated into my worldview, it is likely to affect some if not all other premises that support it.

If I insist on maintaining my original assumption, I am vulnerable to any variables that I refuse to recognise – I may well get knocked down as I confidently stride across the road.

This latter position, in which I maintain my value or assumption in spite of evidence as to its contingency, would be deemed a 'sedimented' view, or more simply, 'sedimentation'.

The road-crossing example is a fairly innocuous one; when applied to assumptions or values about oneself or about the nature of love, for example, the consequences of sedimentation can be costly.

32

THE I, YOU AND WE FOCUS

Knowledge, truth, perception, awareness, self and other constructs are all products of relatedness. Additionally, the process of relatedness has a ripple effect among all dimensions: existence is an integrated whole.

The writings of Ernesto Spinelli (1989) put particular emphasis on the quality of the relationship between therapist and client and propose a model that addresses three realms of relationship: the relationship to self ('I'), to the other ('you') and to us ('we') (whoever that might include). The 'I' experiences my 'self' in the relational situation; the 'I' experiences the other in the relational situation; 'I' experience my 'self-being-in-relation-with-the-other' (Spinelli, 1994, p331–332).

The 'I-focused' realm of encounter is about an individual's experience of being herself in a relational situation. Clients who say things like 'I know I sounded like a complete idiot', 'I wish I didn't find it so difficult to express myself' or 'I really don't think I will ever get a pay rise, I don't deserve it anyway' are talking from the I-focused realm.

The 'You-focused' realm of encounter is about how individuals experience the other and how they experience the other's experience of them in any relationship. A client who says 'I don't think you like me', 'It's obvious you think I'm rather stupid' or 'He clearly worships me' are talking from the 'You-focused' realm.

Finally, the 'We-focused' realm of encounter focuses on how the individual experiences the 'us in relationship' as it unfolds. Typical 'We-focused' statements might include 'It seems to me that we really over-react to each other's statements', 'It feels like we are more in love now than we ever were' or 'I have a sense that we are making progress here'.

In a therapeutic setting, the existential therapist can use their knowledge of these different ways of being-in-the-world with self and other(s) to facilitate the client's appreciation of how they are experienced by an other, how they contribute to this, how the other contributes to this and how this context is the same and different from other encounters. The implications of the dominance of any of the three realms over the other two can be explored and the new insights gained for a wider consideration of the realm/realms that are less favoured.

Any novel awareness of our relational world is likely to affect our entire way of existing. As we have seen, the client has some choice as to how to engage with such novelty: they can choose to deny or ignore it, in hopes of maintaining a status quo in their worldview, or they can enfold these new perspectives into their stance on being-in-the-world-with-others.

33

ANTI-PSYCHIATRY AND THE SOCIAL CONSTRUCTION OF MADNESS

The anti-psychiatry movement opposes the practices of psychiatry and what its proponents view as dangerous and controlling treatments such as electroconvulsive therapy and psychotropic medications. The term 'anti-psychiatry' was coined in the early 1960s by David Cooper, a South African colleague of the well-known Scottish psychiatrist R.D. Laing. One of two central figures behind its philosophy, he didn't actually like the term, which he feared would encourage the development of factions – and fanaticism – within psychiatry. Instead of identifying as pro- or anti-psychiatry, he suggested, therapists should strive to work with the lived experience of the client, respecting their 'symptoms' as the way they choose to respond to their environment, and allowing them autonomy in terms of their treatment.

The influence of earlier existential practitioners such as Jaspers (1986) and Binswanger (1963) can be seen in Laing's (1960, p39) concept of 'ontological insecurity' – a feeling of groundlessness that emerges when an individual is denied the opportunity to develop a firm sense of their own and others' identities – something he saw as being at the root of schizophrenia. Laing emphasised the importance of the inter-relational aspect of existence both in the creation of, and response to, this groundlessness – reminding us that we can't understand one individual's behaviour without looking at the behaviour of those around them.

The second key contributor to the anti-psychiatry movement was Thomas Szasz – though he too questioned the appropriateness of the term, saying he believed neither in psychiatry nor in anti-psychiatry. Szasz was a libertarian who saw mental illness as a mishmash of psychological and medical concepts and not as true illness in the sense that cancer can be so described. In his controversial book *The Myth of Mental Illness* (Szasz, 1960) he argued that mental illness was a moral rather than a medical issue. For him, designations like 'schizophrenia' and 'manic depression' describe sets of behaviours that stand outside the norm and that shock, offend or disturb those with power in society. He accused the psychiatric profession of seeking deliberately to blur the distinction between behaviour and illness in order to legitimise the growing use of pharmaceutical 'cures' and the forcible 'treatment' of people who stepped outside societal norms in some way.

Like Laing, Szasz accused psychiatry's dominant medical paradigm of not taking into account the social, emotional, intellectual and cultural dimensions that may be instrumental in the emergence of a 'mental illness'. 'Illnesses' such as schizophrenia were seen by both of these figures as ways of being in the world – strategies arrived at to help the individual survive in a particular context. As Frankl (2004, p134) later described it: 'An abnormal reaction to an abnormal situation is normal behaviour'.

French philosopher Michael Foucault (1971) and Canadian sociologist Erving Goffman (1961) also contributed to the anti-psychiatry movement, challenging psychiatric practice as repressive and controlling, and highlighting the stigma associated with diagnoses such as schizophrenia as potentially devastating to the individual's self concept. Deurzen (2002, p77) reflected on this when she posited that these diagnoses expose people to the 'risk of a lifelong career as a mental patient', undermining their ability to 'cope with the harshness of living'.

The work of people like Laing, Szasz, Foucault and Goffman reinforce existential philosophy's emphasis on the primacy of inter-relatedness in human existence and remind existential practitioners of the need to give clients the opportunity to articulate and connect with their challenges in an honest and authentic encounter with another human being.

34

LANGUAGE AND EXISTENTIALISM

What is it about finding the 'right' word for our thoughts or feelings that makes it such a satisfying, if not jubilant, experience? Perhaps because, in part, it presents an opportunity to share something with someone, to reveal something to another being that might understand me, and as a consequence, I might feel a little less alone.

But in order to even hope that an other might 'hear' it in a way that serves to reveal something, I and the other must share some understanding of what is being spoken about. It is this that renders human beings *discursive,* according to Heidegger (1962): we share an understanding of patterns of meaning. Polt (1999, p74) elucidates: 'as Dasein, I am characterised by discourse; I am able to deal with patterns of meaning'.

Put succinctly: 'How could we have any absolute or pure thought that is not part of the shared language in which we are already immersed?' (Latham, in Gordon & Mayo, 2004, p86). In this we may appreciate that understanding cannot be *'individualised'* (Cohn, 2002, p46), as it is sourced in a with-world, an existence that is shared. In this sense also, we can appreciate that as an aspect of being-with, language is a fundamental condition of human existence.

Cohn (2002, p46) expands on this theme: 'the world we share with others has meaning for us, "speaks" to us, before words are used'.

These assertions extend language beyond words, to include communication and understanding at many levels. This is not to say that the understanding constructed is total or final: it is a process of understanding, and misunderstanding, for both the communicator and the listener. In this rhythm, it may be noted that language reveals, and conceals, at the same time. What is in focus puts other phenomenon in the background. This may not be purposeful; rather, it is a consequence of the unfolding of language, understanding and communication.

However, as the explicit is appreciated and acknowledged, the background implications may become more significant and more apparent. This is echoed in the idea: 'What is spoken is never, and in no language, what is said' (Heidegger, quoted in Deurzen & Arnold-Baker 2005, p95, by Harding).

As a therapeutic and communicative endeavour, existential practice will be informed by these principles.

In listening to the client's communication, or more appropriately, in perceiving them, the therapist appreciates that the client is part of a larger context, and that context includes the therapist. The ramifications of these multiple levels of involvement are ripe for exploration in terms of how they are experienced, understood, and engaged with by the client. The understandings that are heard by both therapist and client are themselves avenues of reflection and enquiry: as these communications are received, affirmed or refined, the understanding becomes process.

Understanding and communication provide a transitory appreciation of our with-world in all its complexities; language is a means of disclosing this: 'With-being is a web with many strands, each of which is potentially relevant' (Cohn, 2002, p41).

Part 3

EXISTENTIAL PHENOMENOLOGICAL THERAPY IN PRACTICE

In this part of the book you will find a wealth of information on how existential therapy works. In Section 3.1 we examine the foundational elements of an existential therapeutic relationship. In Section 3.2 the key therapeutic tasks encountered in existential therapy are outlined . In Section 3.3 we look at ways of working existentially with what the client presents. Finally, Section 3.4 describes the key competencies required by an existential therapist.

3.1

THE FOUNDATIONAL ELEMENTS OF AN EXISTENTIAL THERAPEUTIC RELATIONSHIP

35

THE THERAPY ENVIRONMENT

Existential philosophy places us firmly 'in-the-world', rather than separate from it, and so existential therapists would readily agree that the therapeutic space is a part of the therapeutic relationship and as such should be considered carefully. However, there are no specific environmental conditions proposed by the philosophical tenets of existential literature, although one might understandably assume that the setting would reflect the worldview of the practitioner: this would be likely to include some consideration for the comfort of the client as well as the therapist.

Unlike some therapeutic orientations, existential therapy does not rely on presenting the client with a neutral space upon which to project his transferential thoughts and feelings. Therefore, the space for existential therapy would probably be professional, but not clinical, and personal but not overly so. As Cohn (1997) points out, the therapist provides the space where the client's personal thoughts, narrations and feelings can be described, clarified and understood. How can a client speak personally in an impersonal space?

Although therapy most often takes place in a room selected by the therapist, there is nothing in existential thinking that prevents it occurring in different circumstances, e.g. in a room owned and maintained by the client, in the open or in public or online or on the phone. Teenage clients, for example, might find 'walking therapy' less intense, while adults who travel frequently might look for a therapist who can offer a range of face-to-face and online options.

If the therapy is primarily for individuals, it is preferable to have seating arranged so practitioner and client are able to view each other clearly: this supports the task of considering the nature of the relationship between them, an appropriate point of exploration. Use of a couch for the client to recline upon is antithetical to the idea that existence is inter-subjective, and that our difficulties in that regard need to be clarified, rather than obscured. However, some practitioners (Medard Boss, for example) see the client lying down as a way of acknowledging the body 'as a sphere of human existence' (Boss, 1963, p62), though it isn't clear why lying down is a better way of acknowledging the body in this way.

It is important to consider the privacy of the client, whether their arrival and departure is subject to observation, and whether this would be awkward for them. As confidentiality is a professional requirement, it is necessary to ensure that the conversations cannot be overheard; note-taking or recording of the session should be agreed with the client, as well as ownership of the materials subsequent to the contract. Existential therapists often have an ambiguous relationship to the idea of note-taking and record-keeping, believing in the value of encountering the client as they are in the 'here and now' rather than basing a session on what arose in previous encounters. The very act of note-taking requires the therapist to interpret their encounter with the client, to ascribe importance to some aspects more than others, perhaps even to formally state their view of the client's position in the world, irretrievably altering the relationship between the parties.

Of course, any regulations stipulated by professional organisations should be considered, as long as these standards are aligned with the ethical position and worldview of the practitioner.

> The spatial and temporal 'setting' for existential psychotherapy remains an open possibility bounded only by the combination of the therapist's and the client's belief-based assumptions and their consequent conditions, as well as any such boundaries as might be expected by professional bodies.
>
> (Spinelli, 2007, p94)

As Spinelli points out, it would be advisable to maintain some flexibility in attitude with reference to as many environmental factors as possible: we are not always in control of the practical elements, nor of the requests submitted by our clients. What is critical is an awareness that alternatives to standard practice are possible and may be more reliable and effective and therefore more ethical than unquestioning adherence to stances that probably originated in other psychotherapeutic traditions with different philosophical foundations (Spinelli, 2007).

36

THE INITIAL ENCOUNTER

Preparing to start therapy has both practical and philosophical implications, but the philosophical ones are less often the subject of discussion.

The philosophical aspect is the preparation of the practitioner: it includes reflection on their readiness for such an engagement, which is also an ethical issue; but perhaps more importantly it demands some consideration of the biases and assumptions that are already present by virtue of the therapist's theoretical orientation, and also as a consequence of the first contact with the client (whether that be by phone, email or in the form of referral notes). The initial meeting between client and therapist continues the process of 'co-creating' the therapeutic relationship that started as soon as initial contact was made. As Cohn (1997, p33) points out:

> The client you meet as the therapist is the client who meets you. There is no client as such. If two therapists meet the same client, it is not the same client.

It is advisable to notice the quality of relationship that has already begun, even before the first meeting: what impressions linger, what assumptions are in play. The phenomenological method can provoke reflection and assist in clarifying and bracketing pre-judgements and suppositions.

The meeting and greeting of the client in the initial session is not subject to a specified procedure: the style of the encounter should reflect the stance of the practitioner. As has been noted earlier with reference to the dimensions of existence as proposed by Deurzen (1997) and Binswanger (Spinelli, 1989), there is a social aspect to situations; how this is interpreted and expressed by the therapist should be representative of their assumptions about what is appropriate to this context. It might also be that what is appropriate with one client may not be so with another. To the extent that one can remain responsive to the circumstances, one may be better able to offer a thoughtful and personal welcome.

The manner in which the therapist listens to the client should not be any different than any other meeting: *what* we are listening *for* and *how* we are listening are the principles in place. The client's worldview begins to unfold at the first utterance: the narrative reveals the significant relationships and issues that are currently demanding their attention. The therapist attends to the client's concerns while maintaining some awareness of their own biases and the way in which the client might be perceiving themselves in the session, any perceptions they may be forming of the therapist, and the way the shared space inhabited by both is being experienced. For example, the therapist may become aware that the client has ambitions to be experienced by them in particular ways: for example, helpless, resilient, vulnerable and/or rational. The practitioner also has intentions of being seen in a particular light: empathetic, professional and/or trustworthy, for example.

These are only beginnings: the quality of the relationship will develop on the basis of the contributions of both – shared and co-created, but not necessarily equal. Both parties are concerned with clarification – but it is clarification of the client's experience rather than the therapist's.

It is probably useful to keep in mind that there is no telling if this pair will meet again: both people have the freedom to choose to return, or not; we are all subject to the vagaries of life that could preclude our attendance. Any encounter could be the last. As such, each session should be regarded as 'the therapy' in its own right, in and of itself.

37

THE ROLE OF THE THERAPIST

The existential phenomenological stance regards each client as individual and each therapeutic encounter as unique. Unsurprisingly, therefore, existential therapists are concerned that articulating 'a way of being a therapist' will result in the application of an approach to working with clients that is rigid and manualised.

Some forms of existential therapy are more explicit about the role of the therapist, than others. Deurzen, for example, describes the therapist as a 'mentor' or 'wise person' who brings a special wisdom and experience to the client's reflections (Cooper, 2003). In Logotherapy, therapists are expected to take charge of the therapeutic process, while therapists influenced by R.D. Laing (1960) will allow the client to structure the session. In Daseinsanalysis, the therapist may focus on the client's maladaptations and dysfunctional ways of being, while therapists who share the philosophy of the anti-psychiatry movement might look for the intelligibility and purposefulness of the client's symptoms (Cooper, 2012).

What is true in all forms of existential therapy is that the role of the therapist will reflect the aims of therapy and the therapist will start by facilitating an exploration of the client's lived experience, that is, her 'worlding' as represented by her worldview.

In a joint enterprise, the therapist and client work to clarify the values and assumptions integral to the client's worldview. Many of these elements would not have been previously reflected upon: the contradictions and relative 'truth' of these perspectives can be exposed by thoughtful review of the client's experiences in conjunction with the attentive listening of the therapist. This is by way of an exploration: an enquiry that entertains questions and values them more highly than answers. This perspective is related to the proposal that truth is never pure, simple or complete.

True to the nature of enquiry, the existential therapist eschews technique in favour of practice. Cohn (2002) makes this distinction clear: he proposes that practice is an 'enactment' of one's beliefs, as opposed to the application of methods or mechanics. As an extension of one's beliefs, practice in this sense allows for the therapist to be fully present and available for and to the client, without the distraction of fitting the client's difficulties into a pre-formulated theory. Additionally, the therapist has a much greater range of possibilities in the *manner* in which they engage with clients, liberated from prescribed interrogation and imposed solutions.

The emphasis is on 'being with' the client: this is in the service of establishing a relationship in which the client can more readily and freely describe their lived experiences. Existential practitioners do not aspire to cures, or even changes in behaviour: rather, they provide a relationship that offers the opportunity for the client to reflect on the nature of their own difficulties, and possible alternative ways of responding to their possibilities of being-in-the-world. Spinelli (2007, p111) describes it as follows:

> The therapist is both the representative of all others who contribute to the definition and maintenance of the client's other-construct and, just as importantly, is also the other who challenges the client's current other-construct and, hence, the currently maintained worldview.

It is the responsibility of the therapist to be explicit about what they are offering in therapy. The belief that it is only the client that can choose how to live their life is a maxim that is better demonstrated than explained: the practitioner must resist attempts to be drawn into suggesting particular changes or remedies to the client's difficulties. In admitting to incapability, as well as unwillingness, to supply the client with neat answers, the therapist encourages the client to regard themselves as the authors of their own existence.

38

THE ROLE OF THE CLIENT

The client should be made aware of the intentions of the therapist; from this basis, it is easier to describe the kind of participation expected of the client.

The therapist might briefly explain a few basic assumptions about their way of working: for example, that they hope to facilitate clarification of the assumptions and values that inform decision-making; or that they are open to expression from the client concerning the relationship between them. It is usually useful to directly address the notion of solutions or cures, as these are not the aims of therapy. Each client must come to find their own, personal way of being in the world and must choose for himself or herself how to face both the universal and the unique challenges their journey presents. Explaining this to the client can open the door to further enquiries from them as to what might be expected of them, and how they can best enter into a process that they hope will address their problems.

Once the process of therapy has started, it is likely that the client will develop an appreciation of what is expected of them, and what does or does not 'work' for them. These discoveries may relate to the therapeutic process itself or to the relationship with the practitioner.

On those occasions when a significant understanding or shift in perception occurs, it is useful to reflect *what* has happened, and *how* it has been a consequence of the client's willingness to reflect and explore, providing further demonstration as to how the participation of both therapist and client serves the aims of therapy.

Additionally, when there are meetings in which the client does *not* feel inclined to participate, this too should be viewed by the therapist as an opportunity to discover with the client what is impeding their engagement; this, again, can illustrate to the client that the quality of the engagement, as well as that of the therapy, is, in part, a consequence of their own contribution.

Finally, it is the role of the client to determine if the therapy is useful; in fact, it is their obligation. If there is an educative element to the therapy, it is in the appreciation of how reflection can clarify, to some extent, the basis on which the client chooses to live their life.

39

CONTRACTING AND BOUNDARY SETTING

It is interesting to note that there are implicit contracts and boundaries in every human encounter: when waiting at a bus stop (in some countries at least), it is considered polite to 'queue' for entry; when meeting someone for the first time, you may be expected to offer a handshake. These kinds of unspoken agreements are the practices of community and cooperation and allow us to manoeuvre our way around society with a modicum of grace.

All of the examples mentioned are contingent: they are flexible, can be readily modified, and for the most part bear no great consequences if breached.

Contracts and boundary setting in therapy, as in life, are fabricated frameworks – Spinelli (2007) likens them to 'magic feathers' based on the feather that the elephant Dumbo, in the cartoon of the same name, believed was the secret behind his ability to fly. Contracts are meant to clarify the rules and conditions of specific settings and meetings and encourage initial disclosure by the client by establishing a framework in which such disclosure feels safe. However, psychotherapeutic contracts are essentially arbitrary, with all due respect to the guidelines of professional organisations. They can serve to clarify expectations and intentions, as well as the consequences of non-adherence. They can, to some extent, mitigate the anxiety inherent in every human encounter, but certainly that tension can never be eliminated: everyone party to the agreement can change their minds, even without warning. In this way, the counselling contract is very similar to all other commitments.

The contract sets out the practicalities of the sessions, e.g. dates, times, confidentiality, durations, payment, absences, and any other stipulations that client or practitioner deem necessary (for example, no smoking in the consultation room). If there is an agency involved, there may be other conditions required for their specific agenda – for instance, abstention from illegal substances. Additionally, professional registering bodies have requirements or suggestions for contracting, and there are statutory requirements for the profession that must be considered.

Boundaries are the more overtly flexible elements of the contractual agreement. These might include policies around contact outside of scheduled session time, relationships with other health care professionals or the reading or review of written materials.

The boundaries and elements of the contract will be subject to discussion throughout the therapeutic work: in fact, the contract and boundaries set by agreement between therapist and client are themselves an integral *part* of the therapeutic process. They offer both parties an explicit opportunity to acknowledge their values and expectations, and to enter into negotiation to realise these. Almost inevitably the conditions set out at the commencement of therapy will be subject to breaches, inadvertent or intended, and will demand modification for a variety of reasons.

This process is a reflection of what happens in life: we make agreements and commitments; then things change, people change, and we have to decide how to respond to novel demands and needs, for ourselves and from others. The critical point is that whatever the agreed contractual conditions and wherever any changes to the contract originate, both parties must be involved in their construction, deconstruction and reconstruction.

40

ASSESSMENT FROM AN EXISTENTIAL PERSPECTIVE

The term 'assessment' does not fit easily with the existential attitude: it would be difficult to indicate what is being measured, as the human being is ultimately unknowable, and is changing constantly. Cohn (1997, p34) points out that there is no such thing as a client's 'history' because this history is disclosed in the process of interaction with the therapist in a way unique to that interaction. For him, therefore:

> This means that there cannot be an 'assessment' as this would imply an objective situation independent of time, place and the contribution of the assessing therapist.

A formal assessment immediately establishes the therapist as leader of the therapeutic endeavour and establishes his/her worldview as dominant and he/she as the 'expert' in the therapeutic process. Also, by attempting to isolate particular aspects of a client's worldview through formal assessment, we inevitably distort that aspect and lose its significance, which can only be divined from exploring the wider situation of which it is a part.

The initial or introductory meeting is an opportunity, however, to discover whether the two people involved are willing to work together. In this meeting, the existential practitioner explains their perspective on therapeutic work and contracting: this is likely to elicit queries from the client about the suitability of the work, and of the practitioner, with reference to the kind of assistance they are seeking.

This meeting is likely to be anxiety-provoking for both parties, as first encounters in life are also fraught: both people involved are considering their own safety; concerns about acceptance, validation, support and even congeniality will be foremost. It isn't necessary for the two people involved to *like* each other, but it is necessary to consider whether they are willing and able to *hear* each other.

The anxiety of this first encounter can be productive, and may be illustrative of the relational issues that are problematic for the client. The anxiety of the therapist is indicative of the nature of relatedness and choice: it is the responsibility of both people to choose to continue the work together, or not. This is a question that can be posed at the conclusion of the session: either or both parties may decide to consider it before scheduling further appointments.

The therapist is likely to enter into this encounter in the very same way they would any session: with the attitude of attention and presence. By virtue of this, it may be considered a 'work' session. It is a common practice to enquire as to the client's expectations; this may be counterproductive as it seems to foster a fixed perspective on an inherently creative process. Choosing to enter therapy on the basis that it makes very few promises other than exploration can be daunting, but it is very like the uncertainty that confronts us with any commitment.

Assessment in the sense that it is used in existential therapy can be seen as the opportunity to consider and re-consider one's choice, particularly against the backdrop of time, and therefore is an integral part of the therapy, not just a one-time event.

41

THE AIM OF EXISTENTIAL PSYCHOTHERAPY

Although most existential practitioners are resistant to attempts to define their approach too rigidly, there is general consensus that the global goal of existential therapy is 'helping clients to live more satisfying and fulfilling lives through facilitating their ability to live authentically' (Cooper, 2012, p50). Of course, there is disagreement as to what an authentic way of living looks like and the aims of existential therapy vary depending on the particular stance the practitioner takes. A therapist whose perspective focuses on the relational aspect of existence, for example, may want to help the client to explore their way of being in the world with others. Practitioners more influenced by Frankl (1980) and the tenets of Logotherapy, on the other hand, might encourage the client to identify what gives their life meaning and shines a light on their particular project in life. Those who are strongly phenomenological in their approach may be wary of setting any goals at all, outside of those established by the client. Despite coming from different starting points, however, most existential practitioners would agree that their broad aim is to assist the client in exploring their worldview, and to help the client to clarify the effects of the worldview as it discloses their engagement with the givens of existence.

The givens of existence fall into two categories: the universal conditions that every human encounters, like temporality, death, freedom, etc., and the 'givens of circumstance' (Cohn, 2002, p45), which are those aspects of our past that are the consequences of 'throwness', e.g. our parents, our nationality, our physiological traits; 'throwness' in turn also includes our history and the consequences of our previous choices.

In the course of reflection on the worldview of the client, as the possibilities and liabilities of the worldview become clear, the client can decide if and how their responses to the givens might be modified. Very often clients have difficulty distinguishing between those things that they can change and those that they cannot. An example of this may be anxiety: existential anxiety is a condition of life, and our response to it is where we may exercise our freedom; the client who wishes to be free of anxiety would also have to be relieved of living and choosing, a rather self-defeating option.

For the existential therapist, symptom removal or cure is not the purpose of the process; in fact, the problem, or symptom, is a necessary indicator, as it points the way to the issue at the heart of the dilemma. A client who seeks help with his phobia of vomiting may decide, having examined both the positive and negative consequences of his phobia, that he is no longer interested in ridding himself of it, but rather feels able to embrace it as a part of his worldview that it benefits him to retain. Shifting his attitude to the phobia in itself contributes positively to his wellbeing.

All aspects of the worldview are inter-related: clients try hard to maintain all the components of their worldview, therefore, a modification in any of them will have far-reaching consequences. The benefit of the existential-phenomenological process is found in the client's new awareness: their ability to recognise the losses and the gains in their chosen response to the human predicament. These effects impact on the client themselves, and the entirety of their world: the same can be said for any alteration in perspective and behaviour.

It is for these reasons that the therapist seeks to come to some understanding of the client's difficulties, in conjunction with the client, before reviewing options for change. As highlighted above, frequently the new awareness or perspective *is* the change, without apparent modification of behaviour: the client has a more profound appreciation of their strategy that underpins their choices, a sense that they are responsible for those choices and an understanding that they could choose differently if so inclined.

42

THE CENTRALITY OF THE THERAPEUTIC ENCOUNTER

The existential therapist focuses principally on *how to be*, instead of on *what to do*. The therapeutic encounter is seen as an opportunity for reflection rather than a place for the client to have their behaviour, thoughts or feelings analysed and labelled, and their causation determined.

In being-with the client, the therapist allows the relationship to become a secure and safe context in which the client's ways of being-in-the-world are disclosed. The therapist is concerned only with the revelation and unpacking of the worldview, and accepts it in its current formation; there is no intention to modify the perspectives, they are accepted as the client's lived reality.

The presence of the therapist as the *attending other* allows the exposure of the client's perspectives on relatedness: their assumptions and expectations of how they are perceived, how they perceive others and how they experience themselves in relationships. As the relationship develops between client and therapist, the acceptance and reception of the client's experience by the therapist fosters trust: the client is likely to be more willing to review their perspectives, the ways in which they deceive themselves or live contrary to their own values and expectations, on the basis that they do not need to defend or rationalise things. Through the adoption of a dialogical attitude, the therapist encourages her clients towards a 'truthful dialogue' (Farber, 2000) with themselves and between themselves. All aspects of their being are explored – emotions, beliefs, values, thoughts, ideas, actions, etc. – and seen as being part of a dynamic whole (Cooper, 2003).

As the 'present other' (Spinelli, 2007), the therapist represents all others that populate the client's world: the client–therapist relationship is similar and dissimilar to these other relationships. The *how and why* of these differences and similarities can assist in the clarification of the contradictions and ambiguities in the worldview, and its various aspects.

The immediate experience of the therapeutic encounter is a powerful inroad to comprehending the client's perspective. An examination of the expectations and assumptions with reference to the therapeutic relationship, and contrasting it with what is actually being experienced by the client, can foster a re-consideration, if not a modification, of these attitudes. In any case, the client is challenged by the very existence of the therapist, and investigations into the qualities of the encounter are central to the revelation of values and suppositions. Yalom (1980, p91) reinforces the importance of the living moment of the therapeutic encounter when he states:

> It is the relationship that heals, the relationship that heals, the relationship that heals.

Staying with the client, or being with the client in an attitude of naïveté grants the client the space to hear themselves, and challenge themselves: in the absence of a force that intends to change them, if even for their own good, the client finds themselves in the situation of responsibility. Assuming the therapist is willing to be open and transparent about the relationship, the therapeutic encounter can also demonstrate for the client an authentic model of living.

The clarificatory and descriptive investigation facilitated by the practitioner's being-with is in fact the work that is to be done. Whether the client chooses to maintain their assumptions, modifying some or all of them, is not the concern of the therapist: the hope of the therapist is that some appreciation of agency on the part of the client is a noteworthy consequence of their work together.

3.2

KEY THERAPEUTIC TASKS

43

EXPLORING THE FOUR WORLDS

The four worlds or dimensions of existence are a model for orienting our perspective on human existence – a way of plotting a person's position in the world that is descriptive instead of prescriptive (Deurzen & Kenward, 2005). Existential practitioners don't use the four worlds in an overt way, nor do they question the client directly about their experience of any of the dimensions. Instead, the client's stance towards each of the dimensions is explored as and when the client raises elements of them.

The Umwelt or physical world: In this dimension, we encounter the world in all our physicality, and all that this implies. The main struggle here is around the search for dominance over the elements (as in technology or sports) and the need to accept the limitations of natural boundaries (including old age or ecology) (Deurzen & Adams, 2010). The definitive poles are life and death, health and illness, pleasure and pain. With our body, we act and inter-act with our environment, and all the elements contained therein, including other people. Our senses give rise to perceptions; we seek to 'use' those objects we perceive as tools to provide safety and comfort. Exploring clients' physical worlds may reveal their struggles to create and maintain physical safety for themselves, their sense of mastery or lack of control over their body, their fear of ageing or their tendency to deny their physical needs.

The Mitwelt or social world: We are entities engaged with other entities – this is the realm of the social world. Intimate relationships don't fall into this category alone – they extend also into the personal dimension. This dimension is concerned with 'the everyday encounters' that are part of our public world (Deurzen, 2002, p68). Some of the polarities here are:

belonging and isolation, love and hate, acceptance and rejection. In this sphere, we seek to communicate our values, and to achieve the realisation of these with the collaboration of others; if this is impeded, we stand in conflict with others. Communication occurs in this realm as the means by which we access society, and foster cooperation. Aspects of the social world that might feature in therapy include clients' feelings about other people and their motives and intentions, the sense of separation and fusion clients have with intimate others, the ways in which they relate to others (through dominance or submission, for example) and the extent to which they feel lonely or crowded in their social world.

The Eigenwelt or personal world: This dimension concerns the personal and private sphere and is that aspect that includes selfhood, our character, past experience and physical possibilities (Deurzen & Adams, 2010), as well as feelings, character traits, ideas and aspirations. Some of the poles in this realm are identity and confusion, perfection and imperfection, confidence and doubt. This is the arena of intimacy, belonging and ownership: although we are always in relation, this is where we experience privacy, and a sense of what is known and recognised. In this sphere we appreciate our strengths and weaknesses, our limitations and potentials. Those closest to us are placed in this realm as we experience a sense of intimacy and safety with those individuals. Explorations of this world centre around the client's sense of self, their perceived strengths and weaknesses, their level of confidence, their responsibility towards others, the way in which they approach the universals of freedom and choice, their feelings of belonging or difference and their vulnerabilities as a person.

The Überwelt or spiritual world: This is the realm of meaning and purpose, and concerns the unknown and our sense of the structure of existence, our relationship with our beliefs or values. For some people this dimension is about religion, for others it is about spirituality or values. Examples of the polarities in this dimension are meaning and absurdity, purpose and futility. This is the category of ultimate values and ideals. This is often the world most outside our clients' awareness.

Our values, beliefs and ideals tend to be incorporated in our worldview – something that we rarely dismantle or consider explicitly. Recognition of our spiritual world is considered somewhat outdated, even whacky, and as a result many of us have thrown out our ideals together with our religions, and people's values are often muddled and confused (Deurzen, 1998). It is important to pay attention to this world as part of the therapeutic endeavour. A key aim of existential therapy is to enable the client to illuminate and confirm their ideals and values and to live their life in line with them. When a person expresses interest in how existence, the world at large, or the cosmos is organised or meaningful, these are themes associated with the spiritual realm. Here, we can discern how the person makes sense of the world in a way that gives a structure to all corresponding realms.

In dialogue with the client, the therapist listens for which of the four worlds has prominence in the moment, and which of them are neglected or relegated to the background. The intent is not equilibrium or balance among them, but rather a reflection on what is emphasised and de-emphasised and what that says about the client's worldview and way of being.

44

MAPPING THE CLIENT'S WORLDVIEW

Our worldview consists of our attitudes, expectations and assumptions with respect to self, other and the world. By imposing this structure of meanings, beliefs and values upon the world, we seek to make sense of it, to fix it in ways that we can predict and rely upon. Without a worldview, we might be thrown into a maelstrom of anxiety and despair by the reality of a world that is constantly changing and in which nothing has inherent meaning.

As Spinelli (2007, p23) points out, our worldview 'provides the basic structural means through which the full impact of the inherent uncertainty accompanying the experience of worlding can be partially withstood and allayed'. The way a client constructs their worldview, therefore, is of great relevance to the therapeutic process as it offers some understanding as to how they are choosing to engage with this inherent uncertainty at that particular moment in time.

The client able to reflect on how she responds to the givens of existence will also have the opportunity to modify this response, or to *choose*, again, their current strategy. For example, she may state categorically and with absolute certainty that she could never cope without the knowledge that she has at least six months' salary in her savings account. She may be convinced that without this safety net she would be so terrified of the prospect of financial hardship (and the loss of her home and independence she feels certain would be the result), that she would simply be unable to survive. Therapeutic examination of the way in which she is responding ontically to the ontological reality of an uncertain future may highlight ways in which her strategy restricts her – by preventing her from embracing opportunities to travel, or stopping her from launching a longed-for new business that may provide her with a fulfilling vocation, for example. These realisations may encourage her to take a different stance to her financial situation and therefore to alter the element of her worldview that deals with anxiety and the unknown. Alternatively, she may decide the losses inherent in her stance are a price worth paying for the perceived benefit of 'peace of mind' and 'security'. Either way, the exploration allows her to take responsibility for a choice that she is now able to make in full cognisance of all its implications – both positive and negative.

The ontological aspects of existence are demonstrated in our ontic responses. Often exploring our ontic responses to things can be deeply challenging and anxiety-provoking. This is because the process threatens to expose the cracks in the meanings that we assign to things, meanings that are 'worldview's attempt to structure worlding' (Spinelli, 2007, p26) – in other words, are our way of making sense of what happens in the world in general and what happens to us in particular. As a result, we can be very resistant to any attempts to challenge our deeply fixed or sedimented meanings – even to the point where we ignore or dissociate from experiences that challenge us to think differently (Strasser & Strasser, 1997). A client who interprets their partner's possessive jealousy as 'just their way of showing how much they care', for example, may find it difficult to acknowledge actions or behaviours on the part of their partner that to others clearly indicate a lack of concern for the client's wellbeing. The threat of losing the 'reality' that their partner cares for them, blinds them to the range of alternative meanings behind that partner's behaviour.

The existential therapist must be conscious of the impact that the deconstruction and examination of the client's worldview may have on the client. Such work must be carried out with curiosity and sensitivity and at a pace dictated by the client. The therapist must ensure there is space in the process for the individual to construct and inculcate alternative meanings in the face of a destabilised or broken-down worldview. They must also attempt to 'stay with', 'stand beside' and 'accept the otherness of the being who is present' (Evans, 1981), bracketing their own worldview and the values and beliefs it contains, so as to enable the client to reflect upon ways in which their worldview might better enable them to live authentically.

Precisely how the therapist facilitates the shifts in the client's worldview is open to debate. However, it is generally acknowledged by existential therapists that an important (if not the most important) vehicle for this process is the therapeutic relationship. Of course, all the givens of existence are inter-related, as are all aspects of the worldview: therefore, if one is affected, so are all. So from consideration of the client's stance within the therapeutic relationship, a wider exploration of other aspects of the client's worldview may follow.

This process can be described as a mapping of the client's worldview. The universal conditions or givens – uncertainty, temporality, throwness, embodiment, anxiety, attunement, death and finitude – will be disclosed in the particular manner in which the client engages with and responds to them. This exploration facilitates an understanding of the client's situation: how they are being-in-the-world. The client is then in a different position from which to choose to modify, dispense with or maintain their perspective. This understanding, however, is never final, or total. As Cohn (2002, p57) points out, 'in this kind of therapy, understanding grows, but is never complete'.

45

TUNING IN TO EMOTIONS

Feelings and emotions have long been the subject of philosophical and scientific debate – Aristotle attempted to identify a definitive list of emotions and Darwin speculated that they were throwbacks to earlier, primitive life. Being-in-the-world is being there in *some way*: we find ourselves in the world, attuned to it by virtue of moods, our feelings.

Existential practitioners try not to classify emotions as positive or negative, preferring to see them simply as disclosive, that is, revelatory, of the client's worldview. Feelings are attached to a situation; they are not transferable to another time or place. They belong to the situation in which the client finds himself or herself; they tell us something about their world, and how they are *in* it at that juncture. Because they are neither solely caused by the world around us, nor are they solely outside the world, they are one of the best routes to understanding the client's way of being in the world (Deurzen & Adams, 2010).

Clients often come into therapy in the first place because they are struggling with a range of emotions or with one overwhelming emotion that impacts upon their capability to feel other emotions. However, emotions are not irrational inconveniences that we need to wrestle into submission; rather they are valuable signposts to how we are in the world. Learning to follow these signposts rather than ignore them is a key life skill that allows clients to develop what Buber (1958) described as an I–Thou attitude to themselves – where they are aware of all the different aspects of their being, including their emotions, and can accept them as part of their changing response to the world, rather than as permanent character traits or defects.

Cooper (2012) suggests that, therefore, the aim of existential therapy is less about changing what he calls the client's *primary* emotions (such as feelings of sadness or anger), and more about understanding and changing their *secondary* feelings about these emotions (for instance, feeling ashamed for feeling angry or weak for feeling sad). Clients are often not fully aware of these secondary feelings, or may misinterpret them or deny them. Existential practitioners would argue that emotionality is a unitary dimension of being: the cost of suppressing one emotion is the crippling of them all (Bugental, 1978).

The therapeutic exploration of the feelings attached to any experience helps identify the elements of the client's worldview that are in play. For instance, if the client is angry, they are angry *about* something; when they review what they are angry about, the value(s) emerge. If they are angry about being ignored, for example, it could be because they have a belief, and an expectation, and a value that stipulates that they are worthy of consideration. If this value is not realised, then they are threatened with a loss (of being perceived as they wish to be), and become angry.

In a therapeutic dialogue about emotions, the existential therapist would pose the naïve question: 'What is it about *X* (person, event, idea, etc.) that makes you *Y*?' (happy, angry, sad, etc.). This not-knowing stance allows a great deal of expanse in the response: the answer may be surprising to both parties; and the response is, of course, not a full or final understanding, but the beginning of further enquiries.

As being-in-the-world is a continuous movement, it follows that emotions are also in flux; it follows that one revelation will lead to another. At some point, this direction of exploration will dissipate, and some reflection on the revelations can take place.

The process could be seen as a 'tuning in, tuning out' pattern (Strasser & Randolph, 2004). The 'tuning in' aspect of the enquiry is appropriate when emotion is dramatically demonstrated in the therapeutic setting; the 'tuning out' is the opportunity to explore the meaning and significance of the experience. These facets of the enquiry are not linear or sequential, but are available avenues of enquiry.

Although there are no emotions that are totally foreign to any one of us, it is important to recognise that while we are all subject to being-in-the-world in some feeling state, the context of this is particular to each person. Each one of us has a unique horizon, and although there may be some overlap, it cannot be assumed that any one of us can ascertain or anticipate what another's emotional response will be; additionally, as we are mutable entities, on the way to becoming, none of us can know for certain what our *own* response will be, as every moment is transient, and the 'self' is an unfinished project.

46

PRESENCE, IMMEDIACY AND MOVING TO AN I–THOU

The emphasis in the existential therapeutic encounter is on a quality of being-with: it is this quality that allows a generous space and place for the client to hear himself or herself, and to explore their perspectives.

The safety that is engendered by the attention and the acceptance of the therapist can foster a more open engagement: acceptance does not mean agreement, but it does indicate that all concerns are regarded as appropriate for discussion.

By virtue of the phenomenological attitude, the existential therapist is in a better position to clearly *receive*, that is *hear*, how the client experiences their world. This attitude of 'un-knowing' (Spinelli, 2007) precludes the imposition of theory, authority or the desire to help on the part of the therapist. It also promotes a trust that more readily allows the therapist to invite the client to focus on the current inter-subjective encounter: this challenge can produce dramatic effects. The results of this discussion can then be reviewed with reference to the client's realities in the wider experiential context.

To the extent that a therapist can 'bracket' their own agenda, e.g. the need to display competency or to produce tangible results, they become available to the other in the encounter; this might be called 'presence'. Bugental (1987) suggests that on these occasions, the therapist is more fully 'in' the situation, an engaged participant, and most importantly, an affected participant. On these occasions the practitioner is also more likely to disclose how they are affected by this encounter:

again, this engenders a quality of being-with that promotes honest reflection.

It can be quite a surprise to a client to realise that the therapist is moved by them, and not just by their story, but also by their courage to engage at the depth and to the extent that they are able and willing to do so.

Martin Buber (1958) described at length an attitude of being-with that he referred to as 'I–Thou'. The counterpart to this attitude is 'I–It'. The I–It relationship is that between a subject and an object: distant, detached, lacking in reciprocity. For example, the therapist who thinks of the client as 'being narcissistic' or as 'functioning in the child mode' is regarding him/her as an entity that can be categorised, analysed and fixed. The I–Thou relationship, on the other hand, accepts that the other is unclassifiable and unanalysable as he/she is freely choosing (Cooper, 2003). This relationship goes beyond inter-subjectivity: it is about an utter openness to the other. It requires a meeting in the present moment between the two parties, without assumptions, theoretical models or stereotypes.

This position is ambitious, and Buber allows that it is not possible to maintain the I–Thou stance: it is necessary to operate in the world in a more mechanistic way. It is also impossible to manufacture this event: it is episodic, and the therapist can only be open to this kind of encounter, creating an opportunity for its occurrence through his/her absorption in the present moment with the client.

Existential therapists seek to put aside the temptation to treat clients as 'objects of their experience and self-consciousness' (Spinelli, 2005, p123) that can be moulded, persuaded or educated according to the therapist's worldview. Instead their focus is upon the shared meanings that emerge in the relationship and mutual respect for each other's 'otherness'.

The consequences of such an engagement are that when we are 'known' in this way, and we 'know' an other in this manner, both people are changed. Both perspectives have shifted; there is a different understanding of self-and-other. The parameters of this new awareness are not readily definable; neither are they necessarily comforting. It can be uncomfortable to sit in the knowledge of an other's different values, beliefs and ways of being in the world, to try to hold on to the paradox that we are both totally individual and yet irretrievably in relation.

47

MAKING THE IMPLICIT, EXPLICIT

In any narrative, the participants are not aware of everything that is implied: there is usually a focus on one aspect of the story, and movement towards expanding the meanings inherent in the recitation. As the listener in the dyad, it is possible for the therapist to discern some of the assumptions, values, expectations and aspirations that are linked to the client's perspectives. The therapist can draw attention to these elements, either by making a link between previous reports, or by focusing on the immediate narrative.

This kind of input should be offered tentatively as an invitation to further clarification or correction. Such observations or questions should be in reference to the client's (conscious) disclosures: they are something of a refinement of what has been implied but not directly stated. In all of their interventions, the existential therapist will focus on the present experience, resisting the urge to explain or intellectualise. It is enough just to draw the client's attention to an aspect or element of their experience as they are presenting it.

It can also be effective to bring to the client's attention *how* they are relating their story: emphatic gestures, emotional expressions and the volume of the voice are all communicating meanings that may not be verbalised or realised. To flag up these aspects for the client is to focus on what they might have in the background of their awareness. Again, this is done in the spirit of curiosity, without the application of models and theories, of body language for example, but rather as opportunities for the client to explore.

With such interventions, grounded in the being-with qualities already proposed, there is no getting it wrong: they are opportunities for deeper reflection and clarification. If the therapist is mistaken in their understanding, it opens an unexpected channel for exploration. If the therapist communicates an adequate appreciation of the client's intentions and beliefs, it serves to strengthen the therapeutic bond, and to assist in the clearer recognition of the client's intentions.

It is also a juncture at which the client and therapist might consider the condition of their relationship, and what hinders or facilitates their understanding of each other. Very often the client discloses to the therapist their story in a manner that promotes the client's hopes for being experienced as the kind of person they wish to be. This, too, can be a source of enquiry: the practitioner might articulate this ambition as he/she understands it, prompting a discussion about the client's worldview with reference to being with others.

It is not possible for anyone to be fully aware, in a uniform way, of all the assumptions and expectations they hold: the worldview is revealed only partially at any given moment. As the implicit becomes explicit, there will be shifts, often in modest proportions, in perspective and understanding: this is true for both therapist and client.

48

CHOOSING AND CHANGING

In existential terms, making a choice involves taking ownership of that choice – making the choice knowing that the responsibility for its consequences lies (to a greater or lesser extent) with you, and recognising that you are free to choose otherwise. A client who blames others for making them choose is disowning their choice, disregarding the freedom they had/have, and essentially operating in bad faith. As Deurzen and Adams (2010, p89) point out:

> An underlying principle of all existential work is to introduce, or re-introduce the client to the reality that not only did they contribute to the situation in which they find themselves now but that they can also take responsibility for it changing.

There is no choice without loss: opportunities disappear, we eliminate one option to realise another. Even when the choice seems to be 'clear', or 'the right' choice, the fact that we *must choose* one way forward over another can be a deeply felt reminder that we cannot have it all. Sometimes clients struggle with this reality, avoiding making choices, refusing to make even minor commitments, for fear that they will get it wrong or irreversibly narrow their options. Existential practitioners will point out that even passively not choosing is in fact to make a choice, and potentially results in consequences of equal or greater significance for the client to those they are trying to avoid.

Every choice is made in the face of uncertainty: we may be able to anticipate the consequences with some degree of accuracy, but as our perspective and our knowledge are always limited, there are often contingencies we could never have predicted. In that sense, Sartre suggests, there is no such thing as the wrong choice – it can only be wrong in retrospect, with the benefit of hindsight, but it cannot be made under these conditions.

As with the infinite permutations of meaning, the bases for our choices come down to *nothing*: in so many instances, we wind our way through a maze of reasons and evidence, totting up the pros and cons of every option to justify choosing one over the other; finally, not a lot of it adds up, not satisfactorily. We accrue regrets.

When we attempt to assign the responsibility for our decision elsewhere, we may appear vindicated, but we are drenched with guilt and doubt. When we stand heroically in full recognition of our freedom, we feel the isolation: we are solely responsible. It is no wonder that we approach any significant decision with trepidation: either way, it will be painful.

Clients often come to therapy caught in a situation in which they feel they have no choice. There are circumstances that offer no alternatives: a terminal illness, the loss of a loved one. These factical items are visited upon us: it is only in adopting an attitude and in attributing meaning to these particulars that we can exercise discretion.

In these circumstances, the therapist can explore with the client their response to what cannot be otherwise; these might be existential givens like death or embodiment, or the circumstantial aspects of the client's life situation, like the time or place of their birth, or the consequences of their previous decisions. It is usually helpful to clarify the values and hopes implicated in what is chosen, as well as the expectations that will remain unrealised or compromised. Existential therapy can help clients to make a clearer distinction between what they can realistically choose for themselves and what they cannot.

When clients face a difficult choice, particularly with regard to choosing a different behaviour, it is more effective to consider what *is* being chosen before attempting to modify the current tendency. This helps to recognise what appeal the current choice holds: what values are being realised, what parts of the worldview are being defended and supported. For example, a client who wants to give up smoking may be encouraged to consider what smoking does for them, what benefits it offers, how it supports their values or beliefs, what it helps them avoid, etc. Only once they have a full understanding of what they are giving up, of the risks their choice may expose them to, can they make a true choice as to whether or not to continue down that route.

It is not the therapist's role to speculate on which choice or decision is preferable: instead they must support the agency of the client by simply noting that they cannot avoid making some kind of choice; it is inevitable. This is the consequence of Sartre's (1958) proposal that we are condemned to be free.

The therapist can offer the client the opportunity to discuss the anxieties that attend any given choice or hoped-for change: this does not promise a mitigation of discomfort, but it can help to make the struggle meaningful, and part of a creative effort to live life according to their most treasured intentions and aspirations.

The change that existential therapists hope for is that the client proactively begins 'choosing existence' (Cohn, 2002, p62): this is not a choice that is made once, but one that the client will repeatedly face.

49

CREATING/FINDING A PROJECT, MEANING AND VALUES

Our sense of meaning is rarely encapsulated in one totality, but rather is made up of our values and the ways in which we seek to realise these values. A crisis of meaning is a common experience for many of us: we feel that our understanding of how life should make sense has failed us. When something catastrophic happens that causes us to question all, or the most significant, of our values, we feel exposed, vulnerable and rudderless – questioning the very meaning of our existence, or indeed existence itself. Mental health practitioners describe this experience in various ways – as depression, or anxiety, for example – depending on the dominant affect being experienced by the individual. Colloquially we talk about 'having a breakdown' or, increasingly, experiencing an 'existential crisis'.

It is important to note that these crises are not intra-psychic phenomena: they are occurrences in the world, and of the world. It is in the connection we have with our world that the crisis takes place: no world, no problem.

We take for granted the meanings and values we ascribe to the world: they become a part of the compass that allows us to make our way in life. It is easier for us to exist when we convince ourselves that we are 'here to do God's will' or 'put on this earth to change the way businesses manage their people'. Blind absorption in our chosen meaning can, to some extent, shield us from the notion that the very basis of our existence is arbitrary and that no one meaning is inherently and of itself any more 'real' than any other. However, this comfort is precarious and comes at a cost. For example, if I hold a value that it is important to contribute to the wellbeing of others, then the meaning of my activities would be in realising that purpose. If that intention is not realised, or if it is not appreciated, or has unexpected or negative results, my sense of purpose is dented or perhaps even denied; deflation and a sense of futility can ensue.

Existential therapists work with clients in existential crises to help them make a commitment to a new choice of meaning, to discover a *why* worth living for (Frankl, 2004). This is a challenging journey as the client has to be supported as they face up to the loss of what they previously held as central to their way of being in the world. They also need space and encouragement to explore alternative sources of meaning, which in turn will illuminate their choices – or projects – in areas of their life, such as their career, pastimes, family, relationships and so on.

It is precisely because we are being-in-the-world that a 'project' becomes necessary: I need to shape and affect the world so that it becomes a community that supports me as I support it. I want to have an identity for my 'self', if only to differentiate me from the world and from other beings in the world – ' I am brighter than…', 'I am less abled than…', etc. This search takes place across all the dimensions of existence, but is especially prominent in the spiritual domain. It is in the realm of the ideological that I create from the pool of the other three dimensions a structure that provides a map of existence as I understand it. This understanding, like existence, is not final or total: it is restructured with experience.

When a therapist helps their client to explore the meaning that life holds for them, they will ask them to consider what is important to them, what feels right and what feels wrong in their world, how they value different aspects of their existence. Inevitably, in doing so, they will be asking the client to consider the quality of their engagement with the world. If their narrative is primarily self-referential, there is an opportunity to ask the client how they believe their intentions affect their immediate as well as their global community, encouraging them in turn to recognise that the existence of the world and the person are inextricably bound:

this is an essential aspect in the development of our meanings, aspirations and life project.

The raw material of our values, meanings and projects are culled from the social, cultural and historical milieu in which we are embedded; we create these structures from these elements. They are both discovered *and* created. Ultimately, clients cannot not discover, or create their values or sense of meaning by meditating in a corner; they find them in their engagement in the world. Engagement in the therapeutic endeavour is just one of many places where meaning can be found.

50

CONFRONTING FREEDOM AND LIMITATIONS

When clients enter therapy, they very often feel constrained, rather than free – complaining about their partner 'making them' give up a favourite hobby, or that their lack of qualifications means they will never get a promotion, for example. Or they may feel free but struggle to recognise the limitations to that freedom, insisting that they should be able to 'create any reality' or 'overcome any obstacle' if only they want it enough, work hard enough, make the 'right' choices, etc. Finally, clients may not value the options that seem to be available to them, or may be suffering the effects of what appear to be poor choice(s).

By exploring the reality of a client's assertions about their freedom, or lack of it, an existential therapist encourages them to recognise that there are two ways of operating in bad faith – through choosing to believe that they have no freedom and through choosing to believe that they have total freedom. In reality, all choices take place somewhere between these two polarities, and living authentically means recognising both the freedom and the limitation in any choice and making the choice in that context. They don't have access to all options, can realise only a few of the possibilities, and must witness the demise of other possibilities. The therapist will also help the client recognise that the greatest expanse of their freedom lies in their response to what they encounter, as opposed to the circumstances themselves. They may have had no choice over the way in which their partner left them, but they have a choice as to the way they respond to this eventuality, for example.

The manner in which the client engages with freedom and limitations will contribute to the quality of their life in some way or other: if we refuse the burden and blessing of freedom, we relinquish authorship of our existence; if we rise to the challenge of freedom and responsibility, we expose ourselves to anxiety and culpability. Either experience can prove to be less than satisfactory: we cannot abdicate our freedom, we are condemned to be free; we bear the responsibility even when we unwittingly produce undesirable results.

When clients are considering a choice or direction, they can be paralysed by the anxiety provoked by the inevitability of choice. It is at these junctures that existential therapy can assist them in assessing what is most important to them in this situation, what is worthy of realisation, and what must be compromised in terms of their values and hopes.

51

DEVELOPING AN APPRECIATION FOR THE AUTHENTIC SELF-IN-RELATION

Authenticity is a way of engaging with the universals of existence by resolutely facing up to them, and relinquishing our habitual strategies of denial, avoidance and diversion. To be authentic is, first, to admit and accept that we have choice *and* that we have limitations, and second, to choose (within the parameters of freedom and givens) in a conscious and responsible way – rather than just following the crowd and mindlessly ascribing to a 'ready-made' way of being that arises conveniently from our familial, racial or cultural circumstances.

An authentic self is not about a 'real' self or a 'true' self; these concepts do not reflect the intrinsic nature of human existence in which we are constantly in a state of becoming and never a fixed or static entity. To experience ourselves as 'authentic' is awareness after the fact: we may notice that the manner in which we engaged with a crisis, for example, was courageous in that we did not flee or deny the responsibility and anxiety that accompanied this event (even a joyful event can also be a crisis). To 'be' authentic is not attained by striving: it is a consequence of 'openess', availability to existence.

In addition, the aim of therapy is not to enable the client to 'be' authentic, as authenticity isn't a way of being, and nor is it inherently a bad or good thing in and of itself. For example, a client may wrestle with whether to challenge an illegal practice at work (being true to their values around honesty and fairness, and hence taking an authentic stance, but risking being ostracised by colleagues) or to ignore it (suppressing their values, creating anxiety as a result, but potentially 'staying safe' from criticism). In this scenario, determining whether an authentic stance is 'good' or 'bad' depends on whether it is assessed from the client's point of view (where it is potentially both good *and* bad), from the therapist's point of view (influenced as it will be by that therapist's own unique worldview) or from a legal or moral perspective. The role of the therapist in this case is to help the client to open up to and take ownership of that which presents itself to them (Cohn, 2002), rather than seeking to detach themselves from their freedom and responsibility. If they then choose not to take what may at first appear to be the 'authentic' stance, they are choosing in full knowledge of their options and the implications of these options. Arguably, they are being authentically inauthentic!

Many existential thinkers (including Heidegger) believe inauthenticity (if by that we mean going along with society in terms of what is morally, practically or legally approved of) is a more pervasive or natural state, as we are inherently of the world, and have responsibility for others, and the impact the exercise of our freedom has upon them. It may be authentic to tell our daughter that her new haircut makes her look less attractive, in that it aligns with our value of honesty, but equally it may compromise the value we hold around not causing deliberate pain. In this scenario, a truly authentic choice is hard to define. Perhaps authenticity and inauthenticity is best seen, therefore, as a tension that we seek to manage from moment to moment. With every choice, we have an assessment to make and a decision to take. The existential therapeutic space gives the client a safe space in which to wrestle with the authenticity versus inauthenticity dilemma, and in doing so, to clarify their worldview and the relative importance of the values and beliefs of which it consists.

52

DEALING WITH BREAKDOWNS AND CRISES

Breakdowns and crises are moments of grave anxiety, and opportunity. These are junctures where our defences against the contingency of existence are undermined: we feel and understand that we are responsible for creating our own meaning and purpose, that we are finite in our options and our knowledge, that we are headed towards a future that includes more suffering and concludes in an uncertain death; there is a limit to how much anxiety can be allayed by immersion in busy-ness.

It is important in these episodes that the therapist maintains their phenomenological stance: it can do more harm than good to offer suggestions that are meant to ameliorate the distress instead of working to understand it. The client must proceed through the event at their own pace: anodynes that mask the source of the dilemma will impede the exploration.

It can be difficult for practitioner and client alike to stay with the distress. The reflexive response of any human being to the pain of another is to seek to take it away. Sitting with the client as they experience their pain, helping them to understand its sources, implications and lessons, is the key task of the existential therapist.

The opportunity present in these breakdowns can lead to a breakthrough: the foundations of the client's worldview are destabilised and open to revision. Clients should be encouraged not to deny, explain away or disassociate from the experience that has discredited sedimented aspects of their worldview, but rather to work to accommodate it in some way, to integrate it into a new worldview.

The hope is that via the transformation that is inevitable in these critical circumstances, the client can take a more accepting stance towards the anxiety and uncertainty provoked by the recognition that their worldview is *arbitrary*, and contingent; and as a result be free to engage with life in a more creative manner.

It is not necessary or perhaps even possible for clients to restructure their entire worldview all at once: what is probably possible is the extended complexity (Spinelli, 2007) of this structure and enhanced capability to exist meaningfully in a contingent and absurd world.

53

BEING AND NON-BEING AND THE COURAGE TO BE

If we had no anxiety, if there were no anxiety attached to existence, we would have no need for courage.

The anxiety considered here is the anxiety of non-being: this refers not only to our utmost eventuality, death, but also to the contingency of existence; there is no necessary reason for our existence, no inherent meaning behind it.

Unlike fear, anxiety has no object: fear of something allows for a practical engagement with a defined source. For example, if I am frightened of spiders I can take steps to avoid them; if I fear the dark, I can leave the light on at night. Anxiety is sourced in being and non-being, and as there is no particular focus for this, we are left helpless to do anything about it. Fear and anxiety are distinguished but not separated (Tillich, 1952/1980). Every fear is related to anxiety, but the former is an article of perception, the latter one of awareness.

This impossible situation prompts us to find or create objects of fear because these can be met with determination (Tillich, 1952/1980). Clients may present with concrete, identifiable fears – of dirt and contamination, abandonment, loss or snakes, for example – when in actual fact these fears are artifices emerging from their anxiety, which cannot be pinned down and confronted in the same way. A client with a fear of getting cancer may be consumed with worry about becoming ill, interpreting every blemish, ache or pain as a possible symptom and visiting their doctor weekly to seek reassurance. Curious exploration of their worldview may expose feelings of guilt around unhealthy lifestyle choices in their youth and a deeply held, but unacknowledged, anxiety about their own mortality.

The existential therapist's role in these situations is to help the client to peel off the layers of fear and examine the anxiety or anxieties at the centre.

The courage to be is self-affirmation in spite of the threat of non-being: when we are aware of this threat, we invoke either courage or despair.

In despair, a client may attempt to avoid non-being by avoiding being: by seeking to shrink their engagement with the world to a manageable level. For example, they may refuse to leave the safety of their own neighbourhood or even of their own house, or insist on remaining in a job that they hate, to create the illusion of safety and control. In this manner it may be possible for them to affirm a limited self: but they deny or ignore most of their possibilities. The feigned ignorance of the possibility of saying 'yes' to existence, and all it holds, only exacerbates their guilt and their anxiety: they become anxious about being anxious.

Alternatively, the client can choose to affirm himself or herself, to accept that they are 'guilty' and unable ever to live up to all their potential. In doing so they admit that they owe a debt to life: they recognise this in the call of conscience (Heidegger, 1962). If they acknowledge their guilt, but refuse to condemn themselves for it, this is the act of courage: any other path would lead to despair and a withdrawal from the existential challenges.

To be open to the threat and potential of non-being, with all its attendant anxieties, is to be available for the discovery and creation of meaning. It is because we and our world are finite that we apprehend meaning, and thereby episodically overcome despair and meaninglessness.

The existential practitioner will explain to their clients that courage of this sort does not dispel anxiety: it is an engagement that occurs time and time again. Courage appears in and with the choice to engage: it is not a condition before the act. Our clients need not feel the courage in order to acknowledge their freedom and can take action despite their anxiety. Rather, they need but to acknowledge their finitude, contingency and freedom, looking it straight in the eye, in order that they may live a life of courage and intensity.

54

ENDING THERAPY

Far less is written on endings in therapy than on beginnings. For the existential practitioner, however, an awareness of the finite and unpredictable nature of the human condition leads to a focus on the end of therapy right from the start of the journey. The characteristics of endings in and of therapy can be as varied as those in life: planned or unplanned, by choice or by circumstance, gradual or abrupt, painful or pleasant, to note a few examples. In any case, there will be an ending, as this relationship, too, is finite.

Any breach of the time boundaries, by client or therapist, can provide an opportunity to discuss what kind of ending would be desirable (and it may be useful for the therapist to disclose their feelings on the matter): the enquiry arises from 'How do I/we engage with time given to me?'; 'What do I do with my time?'; 'What do I want this time (to be) for?'. As Strasser and Strasser (1997) point out, all existential therapy should be 'time-aware' from the beginning.

The client's stance towards limitations generally will be reflected in their stance to the limited timeframe of the therapeutic relationship. Clients who refuse to consider the possibility of the ending may also work hard to deny the reality of their mortality, for example. Someone who finds it hard to let go of intimate relationships may be tempted not to attend their final therapy session, leaving the relationship, in some sense, still open to possibility. The hopes and expectations revealed in the client's stance to endings in the wider contexts of their life, and whether these expectations were realised or not, offer important clues as to how the client might seek to deal with the therapeutic ending. It is important to bear in mind that any ending reminds us of the final one: all things must end, all things will change; such reflections will implicate all the existential givens, and how the client engages with these.

What, then, are the signals that designate an appropriate timing or an ending? This query infers that there is a 'true' or 'valid' reason for making a choice, or more specifically, the 'right' choice. This is an article of bad faith: our information is limited, we cannot foresee all consequences, and we must choose anyway. Clients may seek to dispel the anxiety that meets them in freedom: but in the end they are responsible, in any case, and cannot escape their 'choicefulness' (Bugental, 1987). The existential therapist will support the client in recognising this, helping them to be mindful of the ending of therapy, and the freedom and limitations that make up the context in which they can choose this ending, right from the very first meeting.

Ending work with a client can be a time for optimism, sorrow, excitement, guilt and a myriad of different feelings. The loss might be focused on the finality of the dyad: neither person will be in a relationship quite like this again: another person will produce another relationship. This unique contact cannot be replicated: the self-being-in-relation-with *this*-other will never be the same.

However, the client may have realised a broader repertoire of being-with: if the therapeutic relationship has flourished, it will have provided an occasion in which each party finds themselves *differently* than they were before.

3.3

WORKING EXISTENTIALLY WITH WHAT THE CLIENT BRINGS

55

EXPLORING ISOLATION AND LONELINESS

Human existence is always inter-related: fundamentally we exist in a 'with-world'. Paradoxically, however, this doesn't preclude feelings of isolation and loneliness: the distance between others and ourselves can seem like a vast expanse.

What Yalom (1980) calls 'interpersonal isolation' is closely connected to existential isolation: as with all ontic and ontological dimensions, there are manifestations in each life of our engagement with all the existential givens. Existential isolation permeates our being: we are aware, even if in an unreflected way, that we are authoring our existence out of the context in which we are thrown; we are infinitely responsible; and we die our very own death.

Interpersonal isolation is the feeling(s) we have when this condition breaches our defences: we may feel helpless, powerless and inconsequential. Our horizon may overlap with others, but they can never completely see our point of view. As Bugental (1987) suggests, we are 'a-part-of' and 'a-part-from' at the same time.

Existential isolation cannot be eliminated, but it can be attenuated via interpersonal relationships and participation with and contribution to others in our world.

When clients discuss feeling lonely, the existential practitioner will help them to explore the relationships they are involved in and consider how these are being experienced. It is important to hear and understand how these relationships are conducted by the client: are they buttresses against isolation, in which case they are primarily self-serving, or are they attempts to genuinely meet the other in their own predicament?

The exploration of expectations and values associated with relationships, whether they are superficial acquaintances or more intimate contacts, are avenues for clarification. What does the client expect, assume or demand from the other? How might these conditions be communicated, or concealed, or misinterpreted, and to what extent?

More importantly, the review will also focus on what the client feels they can *offer* the other: how can they ascertain what the other wants, needs or hopes for, and are they capable or willing to fulfil these conditions? Additionally, how will they ascertain if they *have* contributed to the wellbeing of the other?

The relationship immediately available for consideration is that between the therapist and the client. This engagement can provide a focus for the discovery of attitudes and assumptions about relating. For example, it is often the case that the client is disturbed by the 'one-sided' quality of the encounter: they reveal vulnerabilities, but the therapist does not overtly disclose their own. Or the client makes assumptions about the therapist: they are empathetic, or accepting and non-judgemental, or supportive. The exact nature of these suppositions is less important than the presumption itself: how is the client creating a safe place to be with an other? The challenge here is: what if these expectations are true, partially true or incorrect?

The existential therapist regards the relationship between themselves and their client as 'real': it is not a replay of any other contact, it is not simply symbolic. Like all other experiences, it is grounded in the current situation. That is not to say that the exploration of this engagement will not shed light on other encounters: this relationship will be both similar and unique, and both facets warrant consideration.

It has often been suggested that 'love' is the most effective, if partial, remedy for loneliness: the definition of love has long been debated without conclusion. However, it can be a very fruitful enquiry for the client who complains of being lonely: what are their attitudes towards love, being loved and loving? How might these be related to their current situation?

Such investigations are likely to come full circle: intimacy has limitations (Yalom, 1980) and existentially we face the ultimate event alone. Extending ourselves in relationships can grant us company and make life meaningful: in this way we may be able to affect the lives of others and find ourselves in good company.

56

WORKING WITH UNHAPPINESS AND DIS-EASE

The hyphenated spelling of the common word for illness hints at what existential practitioners consider to be the grounding for our discomfort and unhappiness: a failure to resolutely address the universals of existence.

When gripped by the senselessness of existence, when we detect the arbitrary quality of meaning, we may become disoriented: we feel 'not-at-home' (Heidegger, 1962). It is this sense of dis-ease that is a consequence of existential anxiety; it is the sensation of being called to account for our being.

Unhappiness is a necessary polarity for its opposite: happiness is a comparative, relative construct. This notion can be useful when exploring with the client what they are unhappy about, as well as what makes them happy, or at what junctures they feel happy.

This is a philosophical discussion: the client may discover their assumptions about what they understand by happy/unhappy. Common attitudes include: entitlement, 'I am entitled to feel happy because...'; permanence, 'I have been/will always be unhappy'; singularity, 'Everyone else is happy, why not me?'; and self-referential, 'There is a problem inside me that prohibits my being happy'.

Additionally, in Western culture there exists an implicit mandate to 'be happy'. Many of us are engaged in what Deurzen (2009, p13) describes as a 'quest for happiness'. If I am not happy, I am defective in some way, or even psychologically unbalanced or unwell.

There are any number of likely, inter-related, emotional consequences, once the state of unhappiness is named: shame,

'I shouldn't feel this way'; resentment, 'I've done everything right, why am I not happy?'; confusion, 'Why am I not happy now that I have what I wanted?'; hopelessness and anxiety, 'How long will this last, and what can I do about it?'.

The collaborative reflection on the client's assumptions about happiness, and dis-ease, is not just rhetorical: the resulting values and assumptions with respect to these themes are being 'lived-out' in the client's life. A client who feels entitled to happiness, for example, will feel depressed when they are unhappy – they will feel depressed about feeling depressed.

How the client's assumptions are manifest is the basis of the therapeutic enquiry; what action to take, if any, is the prerogative of the client.

57

THE LESSONS OF GUILT AND SHAME

Shame is a condition that requires an other, even an imagined other. It is the possibility of being regarded in some way that is beyond our own control: we are subjected to the freedom of an other to define or judge us in a given instant. Even when the evaluation issued seems positive, as in a compliment, we can be embarrassed by the declaration, just because it does not align with how we wish to be perceived in that instance. It is the lack of control in this situation that is disturbing. This is vibrantly illustrated in Sartre's story of 'the look', in which the voyeur peering through a keyhole into the room beyond finds that he himself is being observed and judged.

Guilt is different from shame – it is a state that reflects a transgression against our own values. This breach can be a result of a purposeful act (or a refusal to act), or may be the consequence of an ill-considered choice; in either case, it produces a profound discomfort.

Existential guilt, as a given of existence, is ontological: it is not experienced, as such: it is the lagging behind our possibilities; we can never fulfil all of these, so we are always in debt to being.

As with most emotional experiences, both guilt and shame have positive possibilities as they place us on the threshold of authentic engagement with our freedom, responsibility and capacity for choice.

Shame alerts us to the condition of relatedness: we have concerns over how we are experienced, and devise behavioural strategies to affect these ambitions. Whether or not these plans are successful, we are reminded that we need the other to actualise *who* and *how* we are: the other is either an impediment or a collaborator. The same is true of the other: they have need of me for the same purpose. In this way our freedom is curtailed.

An existential therapist will encourage the client to recognise the insights that guilt and shame offer – namely that the freedom to choose how to live is our own, and it is in this context we are responsible, and guilty.

Once we find ourselves being guilty, then we can choose how to respond to this: the transgression becomes a part of our historicity (Heidegger, 1962). The fact of the trespass cannot be undone, but it can be addressed in our response: this might be an authentic mode of being.

It is the task of the existential therapist to draw the attention of the client to the nature of their response to guilt, and to explore its illustration of the values the client has that remain unrealised, and the cost and benefits of this lack of realisation.

With shame, it is important to point out that as we have innumerable encounters, there is a great variety of possible perceptions of self by other; there are no 'correct' perceptions, and of course any of these opinions can change. It may also be useful for the client to consider when and how they *are* experienced in the manner to which they aspire, and to consider how they might have contributed to this occurrence. It may then become apparent that although we may be partially successful in our attempts to be perceived as we wish, that these events are episodic, and never absolute.

58

UNDERSTANDING AND MANAGING DILEMMAS AND CONFLICT

All conflicts involve aspects of the worldview: they occur because our values or aspirations are being challenged, ignored or impeded in some way.

This applies to 'internal' conflict also, particularly that which involves our concept of ourselves: if a client expects that he will always fight injustice, and then finds himself acting unjustly towards an other, he is left with a conflict between his assumption about himself and the experience of himself that he may find almost impossible to accept. In this event, he must rationalise his action or modify his self-perception.

If the client tries to rationalise his action – 'it was because he did it to me first', 'I was tired and grumpy and wasn't myself' – he is acting in bad faith because he is failing to take responsibility for his freedom in the situation. In this scenario there is much to be gained from foregoing rationalisation and the effort to assign responsibility for his actions to an external or temporary factor, and assuming responsibility. By choosing to explore the situation openly and integrate this new aspect into his self-concept, the client is broadening the range of personal qualities and options he has open to him. Such a shift in this dimension will affect all the other dimensions.

The alternate source of conflict is when a client's expectations are not met or their ambitions are impeded by another person. This could happen in relation to any aspect(s) of their worldview: their beliefs about self, other, world or cosmos that are not being accommodated or actualised. This is a contest between the client and other(s) that will inevitably be resolved in some way: battle, defeat, winning, losing, compromise or a combination of these options.

If the client compromises, it is her values that are compromised: she has to relegate one value for the realisation of another, if even partially. In this way, her worldview remains intact but probably shaken. For example, a client may decide to remain in an unsatisfactory marriage for the sake of her children: this allows her to stabilise her self-concept as a loving parent, but she may sacrifice experiencing herself as a welcome lover. She will probably have the added benefit of serving the moral high-ground.

Dilemmas such as these demand understanding as much as resolution: it is often the case that clients come to therapy (couple and family counselling particularly) in some confusion as to the exact nature of the conflict or dilemma. Existential relationship therapy can help to clarify the values and ambitions that are implicated in the situation, enabling the client to recognise what losses are pending, present or past (Deurzen & Iacovou, 2013). These losses will be relevant to the values the client holds in their worldview: they will be defended against in some way in order to maintain the worldview and the (illusion of) stability that it provides. Therapy allows for the supported dismantling of these defences so that they can be examined and reconsidered, and in some cases sacrificed, even partially, to help resolve the conflict.

Conflict can be valued as an opportunity to clarify what is important to the client; and what they will sacrifice in order to have some values realised. It also presents the possibility of assisting an other in the same quest: we actualise a value in serving another person's aspirations; we are able to provide for another from our bounty and with our power.

59

WORKING WITH PARADOX, POLARITIES AND EXISTENTIAL TENSIONS

The need to take a stance on existential polarities such as acceptance and rejection, apathy and concern, balance and extremes, body and mind, conventionality and uniqueness, reason and intuition, solitude and sociability and trust and suspicion (Wahl, 2003) plays a key part in the formation of our worldview.

The client can have a unique understanding of even the end point of each polarity. In response to the question from one of the authors 'What is the opposite of love?' a client answered (much to the author's surprise) 'power'. This led to a revelatory investigation of this polarity as she saw it.

It is a good thing that we can still be surprised, even shocked, as seasoned practitioners: we retain humility in the face of the wonderfully unexpected attitudes of others. This is why it is more effective when working with polarities to enquire of the client as to how they see winning and losing, effort and ease, power and impotence, for example; and it may be even more pertinent to discover that the client's polarities are not organised in the way the therapist may expect. Discussing where the client is situated on the continuum between any of the polarities gives a profile to their worldview, to their 'life project' (Sartre, 1991), and to what is valued and what is being avoided, and why.

Paradoxes are those assertions that seem to be self-contradictory, but are held as, or felt to be, true or partially true. For example, it is paradoxical that we have to live life to the full while being regularly confronted by our own finitude.

Existential therapy encourages clients to dialectically confront paradoxes such as these. By investigating paradoxes, what has been implicit becomes explicit: it is in these processes that we discover beliefs that are in some way contradictory; this does not necessarily mean they are not 'true': they can be 'true' in a felt sense. Indeed, paradoxes can really only be approached in a both/and way and can't be resolved definitively (Deurzen & Adams, 2010). The objective in discussing paradoxes is not to dispense with them, but to consider the consequences of them in order to get closer to the truth. Paradoxes often harbour ambiguities: there are more possibilities in this state than in dogmatic or unilateral positioning.

Existential tensions reflect challenges we face in tolerating the polarities and paradoxes inherent in existence in areas such as life and death, truth and non-truth, freedom and non-freedom, being and non-being. (The 'non' prefix here is deliberate as it allows for a broader spectrum of opposites.)

The enquiries around these tensions serve to identify how and where the client restricts or curtails living: what extremes are avoided or embraced; where is there a possibility for expansion, or when does the client need to constrict their participation? The effects of such 'paradox analysis' (Schneider, 1999) can be dramatic, as might be expected when working with (seemingly) diametrically opposed positions and values.

60

COPING WITH DEATH, LOSS AND SUFFERING, AND THE POTENTIAL FOR GROWTH

Death, loss and suffering are givens of existence that we are all forced to cope with in some way: this means that these factors cannot be avoided, denied or surmounted; it remains to be seen if they can even be accepted.

There is no treatment for death anxiety: it permeates all of human existence. How we respond to this possibility and eventuality is where we exercise our agency. The arena for investigation in a therapeutic context is how we *live* with this event that we never actually experience but always anticipate.

Yalom (1980) suggests that it isn't necessary for the therapist to *provide* an experience of death and the attendant anxiety: it is the therapist's task simply to help the client notice *how* they are already currently engaging with it.

The occasion of a bereavement, for example, can prompt a discussion about mortality – our own and that of others – and also about suffering in general. The death of a loved one raises questions for the client around the meaning of life, and in particular the meaning of *their* life. Such an awareness of their death can foster an appreciation that there is no 'dress rehearsal' for life, there is but one chance to live *this* life that is given to them (even if there may be life after death). At such junctures, the client stands explicitly exposed to the choice to immerse themselves in living, or to retreat from this challenge. This can be both an exciting and a dread-full experience and clients may need help if they are to avoid adopting unhelpful defences against death anxiety. For example, a client may convince herself she is too special to die, while knowing deep down that death is inevitable and approaching all too rapidly. In the face of this conflict, she may have to do more and more to convince herself she is special, becoming obsessed with material success and accolades from others and aggressively denying any suggestions she is 'normal' like anyone else (Cooper, 2012).

The therapist should not dampen these discussions with platitudes of comfort. Instead, Yalom (1980) proposes that the therapist should 'nurse the shudder' that comes with bereavement, in the hopes of enlarging on a concern that is fundamental to an appreciation of all that life holds. Certainly life holds the possibility of further suffering and loss: every such episode points to the likelihood of further such occasions. How we deal with these circumstances, how we ascribe meaning to them, as well as how we evaluate our own involvement with these concerns are all appropriate themes.

It is important to personalise every occasion of loss and suffering. As with any other event, no two people experience them exactly alike. An existential therapist doesn't expect a client's grief to conform to any typologic stage model of experience, such as that suggested by Kubler-Ross (1969). Feelings of guilt, regret, relief, sorrow and loss may be common, but the proportions and composition of the emotional palette will be particular to each client.

Death is the ultimate loss: there are no further possibilities to be entertained as a human being. However, there are many other losses that are feared, and defended against. Any loss can prompt a review of what there is to lose: loved ones, opportunities, our physical and mental capacities, as well as hopes and ambitions.

Existential therapy can help the client to understand what strategies they use to defend against the losses that are most significant for them, and to question the benefits and liabilities of these arrangements. Too often we retreat from involving ourselves in living in a vain effort to avoid the possibility of suffering or loss. As Otto Rank proposed, the loan of life is refused in order to avoid the payment of death (Rank, 1929/1978).

Montaigne (1958, p389) points out:

> Death mingles and confuses itself with our life throughout.

To shun banal clichés is not to be without sympathy or empathy. But to seek to minimise or explain by means of models or rules the rightful pain that accompanies loss, suffering and death is to deprive the client of a more genuine, authentic possibility of responding to these situations.

61

SUPPORTING THE CLIENT LIVING WITH SERIOUS OR TERMINAL ILLNESS

Heidegger (1927) describes existence as the pathway between birth and death. Clients confronted with serious or terminal illnesses are constantly aware of the tenuous nature of their existence and the limitations of their particular pathway. This confrontation with the possibility of non-being, as Tillich alludes to it (Tillich, 1952/1980), generates a great deal of anxiety and often forces them into assessing and revising the meaning they have ascribed to their life to date. As a result they may seek to reach different potentialities in the life they have left to live.

Existential therapists working with this client group face the challenge of acknowledging and bracketing their own death anxiety while sitting with the client's pain and confusion (Pentland & Iacovou, forthcoming). They may be challenged to answer questions about the meaning of life and death, and may feel under pressure to reassure the client or to help them 'maintain a positive outlook'. They may even find themselves using philosophical theory to distance themselves from the client's pain.

In this situation it benefits the client to have a therapist who is willing to work phenomenologically and authentically, acknowledging their own fears and despair as well as the client's, and pledging to travel alongside that client as long as both parties are able. This stance offers the client the space to process their experience and to consider their response to the unspeakable reality of their situation more freely.

This can be difficult and disturbing work for both client and therapist and can take them into the territory of anger, shame, meaninglessness and vulnerability. It is often impossible for the client to share these feelings with their family and friends, who may be caught up in their own battle to avoid the existential anxiety death's proximity can arouse. In this scenario, the existential therapist's role may extend to helping the client to bridge the 'gulf of denial' (Smith-Pickard, 2009, p141) that can open up between them and their loved ones.

Patients with potentially short prognoses often experience a new sense of appreciation and connection to others (Griffiths *et al.*, 2002). The therapeutic process in this context potentially becomes an even more substantial source of empathy and genuine depth in encountering the other – reflecting Yalom's (2008, p205) stance that 'the antidote to much anguish is sheer connectedness'. The therapist must also be prepared to face rejection and hostility, however, and must be strong enough to work phenomenologically no matter how the client chooses to negotiate the treatment and the progression of their illness, resisting any urge to seek to control the client's emotions.

When working with life-threatening or limiting illnesses, neither client nor therapist can hide from the reality of life's finitude. As Iacovou and Pentland (forthcoming) point out, in these circumstances death enters the therapeutic frame as a necessary but unwelcome intruder, an ominous momento mori (Lee & Loiselle, 2012). Such an intrusion can, however, help the client to transcend the day-to-day minutiae, imbuing their existence with a depth and poignancy previously unavailable to them. As Yalom (1980, p159) proposes: 'Though the physicality of death destroys an individual, the *idea* of death can save him'.

62

USING DREAMS AND IMAGINATION TO ELUCIDATE THE CLIENT'S WAY OF BEING-IN-THE-WORLD

When working to elucidate the client's worldview, dreams, fantasies and imaginative scenarios are phenomena of equal value to the existential therapist as accounts of 'real' events and experiences.

Existential therapists don't take the content of dreams to be hidden representations or disguised intentions: rather, they are the opposite in that they are disclosive of a client's worldview, beliefs, fears, etc. Quoting Medard Boss, a psychoanalyst who worked closely with Heidegger, Cohn writes: 'Dreams are an uncovering, an unveiling, and never a covering up' (Cohn, 1997, p84).

An existential practitioner will work with the client to consider the reported fantasy, whether an imagined event, a daydream or night dream, in terms of its themes, its emotive content, the place and time, the people and objects included and the dimensions of existence. They will also ask the client to consider if there is anything missing or absent from the dream theme or content that the dreamer would ordinarily expect or include.

The course of such a discussion very often results in the client recognising issues or aspects of the dream that are relevant to those in their 'waking' life; further consideration of these may develop and provide useful insights.

Although dreams or imaginings are the domain of the individual, and are 'internal' in that sense, the narrative is always about being-in-the-world in some way, and with some concern. This, too, can be the subject of exploration between therapist and client.

Dreams that are particularly powerful or memorable, or those that seem to be repeated in some form or other (or parts of the dream) can be revisited, and the relevance of the phenomena can be contemplated anew.

Dreams very often include the dreamer as both a participant as well as an observer of the action: it can be worthwhile to ask the client to review the dream from these different perspectives.

As the dreamer and the elements of the dream are interrelated, the therapist may work with the client to examine the nature and quality of these inter-relational factors. This is an avenue of exploration that is pertinent to all reports shared in the therapeutic encounter (Spinelli, 2007), whether they are dream or 'reality' based.

Clients can be reluctant to give any serious consideration to dreams and fantasies. The seemingly chaotic scenario means it is difficult to be definitive about meaning and such vagueness can be unsettling. Clients may prefer to have some certainty about what things mean. Abstract art can produce a similar reticence of engagement: the viewer is challenged with participating in the meaning-construction of the work (Barret, 1962). By virtue of the same concern, clients may be reluctant to discuss their dreams because this flexibility of meaning demands interpretation; there is no absolute or 'right' meaning and the therapeutic interpretation that emerges may not reflect well upon them.

The story told in the dream is the more obvious avenue for exploration; but there is also an opportunity for the therapist to enquire as to what it is like for the client to present this report in therapy. The more obscure quality of dreams and fantasies can require a bit more trust between client and therapist: again, this may be a consequence of the indistinct and ambiguous quality of the phenomena, which some clients may fear will reveal wishes or concerns that they would prefer to keep private.

In any case, the significance of the dream is never finally or totally realised, as is true of many life experiences.

63

DEALING WITH VOICES AND HALLUCINATIONS IN EXISTENTIAL THERAPY

Descriptions of people hearing voices or experiencing hallucinations can be found in a wide range of historical and archaeological sources, spanning many thousands of years of human history. Accounts of such phenomena emerge from all cultures, in all regions in the world, and have been studied extensively from the theological, linguistic, psychological, medical, anthropological and psychotherapeutic angles.

When we talk about hearing voices or experiencing hallucinations, we mean that someone is hearing, seeing, smelling or in some other way sensing something that other people around them are not. Statistics vary, but is it generally accepted that 3–10 per cent of people regularly experience such events. Having at least one event where, for example, you wake up convinced someone shouted your name, or you see the outline of a human face in the doorway, is incredibly common.

As well as being seen in mainstream psychiatry as a sign of mental illness, hearing voices or experiencing other forms of sensory hallucination can occur as a result of organic conditions (clots in the brain or Parkinson's disease, for example) or can be caused by taking hallucinatory drugs such as LSD, or ecstasy, or by excessive consumption of alcohol. However, many people who report such events don't seem to be suffering from any pathology at all.

Voices and visions can be comforting, for example when a client hears the voice of a dead loved one (Rees (1971) describes individuals who experience this as 'grief hallucinators'), or they can be very distressing – when voices criticise or confuse the client, or when they have visions of hordes of insects, for example. Whether they want to hear them or not, voice hearing is woven into people's sense of self (Smith, 2007). Recognising this, an existential practitioner will regard such experiences with an open mind, bracketing their own values and those of the culture(s) in which they and the client operate. They will be examined like any other part of the client's worldview, as elements of that client's strategy for coping with the existential givens, and therefore an important source of information about that individual's worldview.

Existential therapy is a chance for client and therapist to work together to identify how the client experiences the hallucinations emotionally, physically and socially. A client who experiences his voices as 'the word of God' within the context of a worldview that incorporates religious belief may have a very different experience from the client whose worldview is founded on rationality and logic and who becomes convinced that the voices are a sign that she is 'going mad'. The existential therapist will help clients to explore the meaning they have assigned to their experiences and will work with them to identify a range of alternative possible meanings, encouraging them to assess the impact of their meaning of choice on their wellbeing.

Individuals do not exist in a vacuum, however – our clients are beings-in-the-world and beings-in-the-world-with-others (Heidegger, 2003) and so the people around them and the culture in which they live also shape their understanding of visions and voices. Socrates had such experiences and was considered to be a man of great wisdom. Joan of Arc had them and is now considered to be a saint. Ghandi had them and is revered as a statesman and peacemaker. Charles Dickens had them and is considered one of the greatest novelists in the English language; and, of course, murderer Charles Manson had them and is considered to be insane and the epitome of evil.

The contextual nature of their client's experience of visions or voices or other hallucinatory events will be explored and will help the client to identify the impact the context has on their experience. People who live in Western countries are most likely to have their hallucinations defined in pathological terms – e.g. as symptoms of mental illness. Those living in other societies may have them seen variously as spiritual experiences, as gifts that make them special, as signs they are spiritual visionaries, as results of tiredness or emotional distress or as cognitive errors. Regardless of how they are perceived, the practitioner's attitude of curiosity and acceptance towards the client's experiences is often therapeutic in itself. The normalisation of what might previously have been seen as 'symptoms' or 'weaknesses' or even 'gifts', and the perception of them as meaningful to the client experiencing them (Suri, 2010) is often surprising and deeply thought provoking to that individual, and encourages them to develop their own relationship with their voices or visions. Sometimes, in the absence of a 'cure' for such phenomena, this change in attitude is the only freedom the client has.

64

WORKING WITH ANXIETY: EXISTENTIAL, NEUROTIC AND NORMAL

Existential practitioners tend to talk about three types of anxiety: existential, ontic or normal and neurotic anxiety. Existential anxiety is seen as an inevitable and therefore normal consequence of human existence (Iacovou, 2011), sourced in the uncertainty of an existence that is labile, mutating and ultimately unpredictable. As such, it is a condition that permeates all aspects of the worldview.

It is at the level of the worldview that we may discern our ontic responses to existential anxiety: these emerge as 'normal' or 'neurotic' anxiety. 'Normal' in this instance indicates only that it is acknowledged as an understandable and adaptive engagement with anxiety. Anxiety over a forthcoming exam or a public speaking engagement would be regarded as normal, for example.

Neurotic anxiety, on the other hand, indicates a stance that is fixed and restrictive, and very often unacknowledged by the individual. This kind of anxiety is usually an attempt to 'name' the source of anxiety, to fix it with a certainty and label it as an entity; paradoxically, this is exactly all that existential anxiety is not. So, for example, a client may attempt to deal with the existential anxiety caused by the absurdity of existence through rituals or compulsions in an attempt to create the illusion of immunity from this absurdity.

In this mode of responding to anxiety, clients are attempting to solidify their existence, to turn it into a 'symptom'. They may insist that their assumptions about self, other, world and cosmos are entirely correct; adamant that their position grants them access to the absolute truth. In this manner, no novel perspective, no new possibilities, are allowed to infect the sedimented worldview and they are protected from the unexpected and unwanted change. The consequence is that life becomes more manageable, perhaps, but there is little room for creativity, spontaneity or a means to meet the unexpected.

Circumventing existential anxiety limits and constrains an engagement with the universal: it shades our view from a full frontal perspective of the disturbing situation; we must choose without the benefit of full knowledge.

When clients enter therapy in the hope of ameliorating their anxiety, an existential therapist might make it clear that such a goal is not attainable; it may be somewhat more comfortable to understand the problem, but we cannot affect a cure for a basic human condition. The exploration begins with discussing what the client is anxious about; when the client is most anxious; and in what circumstances they are less anxious. The answers may illustrate defensiveness against being found imperfect, or indicate tactics used to avoid failure. These investigations may serve to shed some light on the difficulties, and allow the client to begin to recognise that they have some latitude in how they manage their anxieties.

The rigidly held attitudes, semi-truths, assumptions and expectations of the worldview can be challenged in terms of their impact on the client's ability to live a fulfilling life, or weighed up against other possible perspectives and ways of being. Throughout this exploration, the therapist will persevere in their phenomenological stance in order to allow the client to view their situation from the perspective of the one creating their own quality of life. Fuller immersion in living is the only tonic that moderates anxiety; paradoxically, it is exactly this possibility that can also be the source of the debilitating anxiety: the 'symptom' reveals the 'remedy'. As Kierkegaard (1944, p155) points out, however, 'whoever has learnt to be anxious in the right way, has learnt the ultimate' and it is this that the existential therapist can hold up to the client as an aim for the therapeutic endeavour.

65

WORKING WITH ADDICTIONS

Those who are suffering the effects of addictions often describe the experience of 'uncontrollable' cravings or urges. This proposal places them in a position of diminished, if not non-existent, responsibility. Those who describe themselves as 'addicts' frequently subscribe to a notion that they are essentially defined by this term; they propose that they are a 'something', an essence that is irrefutable and immutable. Again, such a self-objectification denies agency on the part of the person so concretely defined.

The existential view of addiction is less about illness and symptoms and more focused on the notion that 'people can get caught up in ordinary activities when those activities become invested with special meaning' (Du Plock, 2013, p206). If this is our understanding of addiction, then anything that quickly and predictably changes our emotions can be addictive.

The existential therapist approaches all clients with a humility and compassion that is born of the understanding that we are all alike: we are all struggling to engage with and respond to the anxiety that pervades our existence with a modicum of grace and some degree of effectiveness. The assumptions that underpin the worldview, and the strategies that are manifestations of this, can serve to ameliorate the difficulties that life brings, but can also produce 'dis-ease'. Addiction is another of these strategies that can be used to help the client to structure their life in a way they might be unable to otherwise.

One of the ways we attempt to protect ourselves from the lability of our self-in-relation is to strive to become objects: Sartre (1948/1973) describes this as a 'useless passion'. If we can convince ourselves and others that we are a *something* that possesses an essence, we will not be expected to be or do anything other than what is assigned to the capacity of that given object: we will not be held responsible for anything else, and we have no freedom to act any differently. In declaring himself 'an addict' the client gains the benefits that come from that objectification, including potentially increased understanding of his plight from those around him, reduced expectations of his capacity to change, etc.

In taking a humble yet curious stance the existential practitioner hopes to encourage the client to move away from the idea that they are unwell, out of control and somehow not responsible for themselves or their decisions.

Typically, the 'addict' client enquires of the therapist: 'How can you help me?'. Ethically, the existential therapist is bound to clarify with the client that 'treatment' for 'symptoms' of pathology is not within their remit: if the client is willing to consider their way of being-in-the-world – including behaviour that causes them and those around them distress – then the work may commence.

The client must understand that the focus of investigation will be their life in general: it is common for them to request that only the presenting problem be addressed – often because they don't want other aspects of their lives to be changed. By candidly proposing a more general descriptive enquiry, the practitioner makes it clear that any or all of the client's life may be affected. This is readily justified in that the client often describes difficulties that they acknowledge are related to the specific behaviour deemed problematic. This stance does not preclude the amelioration of disturbance or a modification of behaviour; rather, these changes may be byproducts of the therapy, and of existence itself.

It is useful to ask the client to describe the situation or behaviour that is disturbing without using labels like 'addict': this relaxes the attachment to objectification of themselves. Such a recounting of the behaviour often results in the client becoming aware of occasions where they do exercise some choice in their lives (this needn't be related specifically to the presenting problem, but may refer to other circumstances).

This offers an opportunity to investigate on what basis the client feels they are proactively making a choice, and compare and contrast these instances with others in which they feel they have little or no control.

In making their stance clear, the therapist indicates that they have no investment in the client changing their behaviour: that is a decision left to them. Although the practitioner may wish that their clients suffered less, how that might come about, or to what extent, is not their prerogative: nor can they know with any great certainty how this might be achieved.

The aim to change addictive behaviour without or before some understanding of its meaning is usually counterproductive. Du Plock (2005) notes that it is more effective to work with the client to discover in what way the 'dysfunctional' behaviour defends against anxiety: only when that which is defended against is addressed can the behaviour possibly be modified and integrated (Deurzen & Arnold-Baker, 2005).

When a client states that they have fears of 'backsliding' into the undesirable behaviour, there is probably still work to be done on the appeal that the behaviour holds: the choices in terms of benefits and liabilities, and the consequences for the client's worldview in part and as a whole, is an ongoing investigation.

Measuring the outcome of such an endeavour should not focus solely on the addictive behaviour. Fingarette (1988, p121) notes with respect to drinkers that a more flexible means of qualifying outcome is needed: it is apposite to consider 'all the changes that the drinker is trying to make'. This seems relevant for all forms of addictive behaviour – eating, gambling, substance abuse, etc.

However, even if the client succeeds in choosing differently on one occasion, this does not preclude them having to make that choice again, and on innumerable subsequent occasions: our freedom haunts us. To accept that we cannot be certain, even about ourselves, and that anxiety demands some response, is to acknowledge that making different choices does not eliminate dis-ease entirely, and that nothing ever will.

66

WORKING WITH DEPRESSION

Depression is one of the most common complaints declared by clients entering therapy. Regardless of whether the client has diagnosed themselves or has been categorised as such by a medical practitioner, the label tells us very little about *what* or *how* the client is suffering; only that they *are* suffering.

When presented with this communication, the therapist offers a naïve probe: an invitation to the client to describe what it is they are experiencing in a more expansive way. In the first instance, this entails a move from the general to the specific: depression is a situation; how this particular person is experiencing it is the focus of the exploration. This indicates to the client that the clues to their distress lie in their own existence: there is no diagnostic or clinical category that will satisfactorily depict their very personal struggle.

The investigation of how the client feels about their predicament will be the most expedient route to their values and the worldview. The discussion will likely move between the dimensions of existence, the physical, social, personal and spiritual (Deurzen, 2002) as well as between the possible realms of encounter, i.e. the self in relation to the other, the other in the relation and the self-being-in-relation-with-the-other (Spinelli, 1994). Themes that implicate the universal givens of existence will also manifest, and these concerns will be interconnected and overlapping.

In response to the invitation to reflect on their experience, clients may describe thoughts, emotions, physical sensations or disturbances: any of these can be considered, as they are all connected and concomitant.

Generally speaking, the existential given that is most often explicitly referenced by clients who present with depression is that of 'meaning'. Their response to this aspect, in which they necessarily create meaning (even when they select a formatted 'meaning' system from their environment or culture) is often one of denial or rejection of the relevance of any valued meaning: 'nothing matters', 'what is the point?' and 'nobody gives a damn anyway' are frequently heard phrases. In these and similar statements there are indicators of other universal aspects: temporality, freedom, responsibility and certainly relatedness.

The consequence of this attitude is very often that the client withdraws into inertia: social and intimate relationships wither, goals and intentions do not actualise, the self-concept is confirmed in the negative, and they have very little hope for the future to be any different. These developments deepen the hopelessness that is so prevalent in this way of being.

Ernest Becker echoes the sentiments of Otto Rank when he argues that those in a depressed mood are '*as though dead* in trying to avoid life and death' (Becker, 1973, p210). Becker goes on to develop this theme in proposing that guilt is an attempt to deny the burden of freedom and responsibility: it locks down the sufferer into a position of inertia. In terms of temporality, the person so situated turns away from the burden, and blessing, of addressing the future: the past is applied as a justification for refusing to choose, as things turned out so badly.

Bugental (1992) talks about 'dispiritedness': he suggests that the client's reaction to their own grief, disappointment and failed attempts to actualise their values and aspirations can further complicate their predicament and increase their suffering. He proposes that the 'presence' of the therapist can challenge the detachment and inertia of the client, and promote an acceptance of their situation. This can induce an important shift: something becomes possible; a crack appears in the defences against agency and meaninglessness. In being 'present', the therapist eschews the aim or expectation that the client will 'change': this promotes an opportunity for the client to do the same. To directly acknowledge their suffering can assist the client in their understanding of it: this is not an easy process for either client or therapist. We must sometimes sit with and witness the client's distress without attempting to 'fix' it: this demands courage on the part of both people involved.

67

AN EXISTENTIAL UNDERSTANDING OF TRAUMA, AND HOW TO ENGAGE WITH IT

Being-in-the-world and being-in-the-world-with-others are conditions of human existence: we are in the world, engaging in it and with it. At times we may reconfigure our stance by virtue of our actions; but most often we choose and act in ways that sustain our worldview in an attempt to create a modicum of certainty and stability: this is a necessary delusion.

As we are beings-in-the-world, our meanings are found in the world and are relative to our context, our situation. The raw material of meanings is not sourced in an individual's 'psyche' or mind: it is in the context of a being who is social and embodied, that is, the with-world.

Trauma is most often described as a loss of meaning: this references those assumptions, values and expectations that we hold with respect to self, others, the world and the cosmos. A rupture can occur in any of these worldview dimensions, and such a breach will affect other aspects. If any of these assumptions is fragmented, we stand exposed to meaninglessness, and the anxiety that attends the realisation that there is 'nothing' in it; there is 'nothing' in us. The constructions we use to buffer the contingency of our existence are revealed for what they are. In this sense, the trauma *reveals* the anxiety that is inherent in existence, it does not *create* it.

When our illusions of safety are undermined in this way, we understand that we never were actually safe from the anxiety of the possible non-being of everything; never were, never are, never will be. We may experience a hopelessness that we may never be able to function again as 'normal', as our vulnerability becomes an overwhelming concern. This realisation can have a profound effect on our self-concept: we do not recognise who we believed ourselves to be, and the direction of this change in us is uncertain.

Clients who have experienced this rupture or fragmentation are often overcome with anxiety, unable to make sense of the world or of the event that precipitated their crisis (Barnett, 2009). In these circumstances, an existential therapist would postpone asking the client to tell their story or describe their worldview, recognising that they need first to 'put on the brakes' (Rothschild, 2000, p102). Instead, the therapist can encourage the client to reflect on their embodied experience and help them to develop their ability to protect themselves from overwhelming feelings by, for example, focusing on experiences, activities or events that bring calmness, and learning to use these reflections in times of over-arousal.

Our worldviews are inter-relational constructs: in this sense, the experience of vulnerability that occurs is also situated in the in-between. Bracken (2002, p148) comments: 'If trauma is about broken meanings, then it is a social phenomenon through and through'.

The description of trauma and its effects as a socially embedded phenomenon has implications for how this situation is engaged with in psychotherapy. Intra-psychic models for dealing with the affects of trauma cannot effectively address the socially attributed significance of a critical situation, and its after-effects: therapists must look to the social and cultural milieu of the person involved.

Once the client is confident that they can manage the distressing emotions evoked by their trauma, the therapist will work with them to explore their very personal and particular stance towards their own experience; and this would, of course, include the social, spiritual, personal and embodied dimensions of their existence.

As all of our experiences are subject to the invariables of perception (the 'what' and 'how' foci of intentionality that allows for a wide range of meanings to be assigned to any experience) there is no experience that can be designated as inherently 'traumatic' (Bracken, 2002). There are many considerations included in the assignation of meaning to the event (bearing in mind that the event can be a realisation, or a new awareness of something). This is not to denigrate any attribution of meaning: it is, rather, a hopeful situation in which the flexibility of meaning allows for change. A client who seeks therapy following the collapse of the building in which they worked, for example, may come to see meaning in the camaraderie and sense of community that they experienced following the event.

The hope would be for the therapist to provide an opening for the client to express, to the best of their ability, how they are affected by the event: what it means for the values and expectations that have so far underpinned their worldview, what it means for their perspectives on the past and the future, and how this event and the consequent understandings might be integrated.

Otto Rank proposed that birth was the template for all traumas: this proposal suggests that it is an experience that is possible, if not inevitable, for any of us. It is this commonality that can facilitate an understanding, if only a partial one, of another person's situation in crisis. As Stolorow (2007, p50) describes it, this 'existential-kinship-in-the-same-darkness' provides a relational context in which the experience can be explored and shared by therapist and client.

68

AN EXISTENTIAL PERSPECTIVE ON SELF-HARM

On close inspection, it would appear that we all indulge in some form of self-harm: we drink too much; don't exercise enough; we are workaholics. These are a few of the more socially acceptable activities that are deemed not to be in our own best interests: but why do we persist in these activities at all? And what is the purpose in or behind these sorts of acts, as well as those that are patently more extreme and aggressively harmful?

We are all subject to the same existential givens: in this regard we are all the same. Each of us responds to these givens in our own way. The strategies we employ to avoid and/or engage with the existential conditions are reflected in our choices, and consequently in our behaviour. All behaviour is therefore purposeful: it is future-oriented, in that it is an intention to actualise our values, support our strategies and maintain our worldview.

To this effect, Jean Paul Sartre proposed that we cannot choose for the worse in any case (Sartre, 1943): we always choose to support our project(s) in some way. This principle can be a guiding light in exploring with a client the purpose(s) of their self-harming behaviour. It is also more effective to consider what *is* being chosen, instead of what alternatives might appear to be preferable on first inspection.

Any activity, or choice of behaviour, can be examined by the therapist and client in light of what purpose it serves: What value is being realised for the client? What self-concept is being promoted? How does the strategy affect other people in the client's life? Is this the desired effect, and if so, how does it serve them? If not, how might they modify their behavioural strategy?

A client who refuses to eat enough to sustain a healthy weight, for example, may find such an examination eventually reveals their desire for independence from anxious and controlling parents. By taking control over their diet, they are stating (albeit in a physically harmful way) that they seek freedom and self-determination. Alternative ways to achieve this end can then be explored by the client and their pros and cons identified, leaving the client with an awareness of the current and alternative choices available to them.

The existential practitioner doesn't seek symptom removal: symptoms are seen as strategies to deal with the givens. These strategies may be successful in attenuating the anxiety, for example, and for some time; or they may be inadequate in a novel situation or crisis. Spinelli (2007) suggests that every so-called symptom is an attempted solution to the chaos and anxiety inherent in the human condition.

It seems that very often the practices of self-harm are executed in the physical realm of existence: the behaviour is self-inflicted physical damage. It would appear that the person is attempting to somehow manage their embodiment. The self-harm may be a way to curtail or enhance the individual's contact with the world. In these ways the strategy is a reflection of one's worldview with respect to self, others and the world. These realms of inter-relatedness are ripe for reflection and exploration in considering the significance of any behaviour or choice.

We cannot anticipate or control how we suffer: we only know that we have done so in the past, and will again. This uncertainty can foster numerous responses: some rebellious, some magical, some attempts at counter-control. The distress inflicted on oneself is controllable to an extent that the suffering visited upon us is not: this tactic can serve in any of the latter intentions. We can rebel against the cosmos, and deface the vessel given to us; we can maximise the endurance of pain by exposure to manageable stress; we may inflict pain and self-mutilation on ourselves in the hope that the cosmos will be appeased by this sacrifice, and spare us the truly unendurable.

The objective of existential therapy in cases of self-harm is to discover with the client how this behaviour satisfies their project(s), to what extent, at what cost, and how the choice of another strategy will affect their purposes. Even in those instances in which the client purports to have no control over their behaviour, there is scope to consider what their options are, even if it is limited to reviewing their attitudes towards their suffering.

69

USING PHILOSOPHY TO INFORM WORK WITH SUICIDE AND SUICIDAL IDEATION

Albert Camus dramatically depicted the absurdity of human existence, beginning his essay *The Myth of Sisyphus* (Camus, 1955/2000) with the proclamation that the only philosophical problem worth considering is suicide. He goes on to declare that the ultimate act of rebellion against a state of risibility and meaninglessness is to live, and to live *more*, not less. Suicide is to admit defeat by both life *and* death; to live with absurdity is to be aware of, and ultimately reject, death.

The person who believes they cannot find the courage to continue living is generally considered to be in despair. They feel hopeless: they suspect they will always feel this way; and they feel helpless, they believe that they cannot help themselves. They are sceptical that anyone else can either.

The nature of despair is difficult to define: it is, as John Heaton (2009) proposes, a way of living, much like passion, or love. It is therefore important to discover with the person in despair and contemplating suicide what it is they are enduring, and experiencing. As it is a manner of existing, of being, the communication of despair will be 'indirect'. Heaton makes the analogy of understanding a joke: the comprehension is more than literal, and it appears in relationship between people who are tuned in to each other.

This exploration requires the therapist to suspend objective knowledge, and assumptions, and attend very specifically to the discovery of the client as they reflect on their experiences. The 'truth' about despair lies with the client: it is their truth.

However, it must be noted that we are all in despair, in one way or another. Tillich (1952/1980, p56) goes so far as to declare that 'all human life can be interpreted as a continuous attempt to avoid despair'.

As outlined by Kierkegaard (1849/1980), despair has two modes: one wills *not* to be oneself; one wills to be oneself. These states represent the poles of the finite and the infinite: at one end we yearn to be freedom and possibility without limits; at the other, we chafe at our throwness, our particular situation, culture, history and the limitations imposed by previous choices. We want it all to be otherwise.

There is no therapy for either of these modes of despair: it is an incurable condition. It can, however, be worked with if the practitioner allows themselves to be with the client as a witness, a participant, and as someone who may not understand or agree with their perspective but who can truly accept it.

It is Kierkegaard's position that those of us who do not recognise that we are in despair already are those that need to be helped in recognising this: only then, from a point of what one might describe as the deeper despair, can we hope to be recalled to the project of living. Heaton (2009) poignantly states that it is 'only when the client sees that the therapist is indeed useless that they start recovering'. It is at this juncture that the client may recognise that they themselves are the source of the despair. With this awareness, they recognise their responsibility.

When determining the seriousness of the client's inclinations, and deciding what practical interventions are called for, it is important that the therapist take whatever precautions are necessary for them to work ethically and within the framework specified by their accrediting body.

The existential therapist will be mindful of the 'in-the-world' nature of suicide. Suicide is not a private matter, but rather something that plays itself out in the world and impacts on friends, family, people who investigate the circumstances behind it, etc. Delving into this situated aspect of suicide and helping the client identify the meanings it might have for those they leave behind can encourage them to recognise that they would be choosing not only for themselves but for others if they were to take their own life.

Ultimately, it is not the therapist's clinical or psychological knowledge that helps the client: it is their stance that reminds the client, and serves to reveal, that we are each and all subject to the same conditions of existence: we must make our own way, in the company of others.

3.4

KEY COMPETENCIES OF THE EXISTENTIAL THERAPIST

70

DEVELOPING A PERSONAL EXISTENTIAL THERAPY

Cohn (1997) suggests that there is a phenomenological dimension to all existential psychotherapy; existential therapies that favour phenomenology demonstrate a proclivity to focus on the ontic dimensions, while those that are less phenomenological emphasise the ontological relevance of a person's existence. Either perspective, grounded in the key tenets of existential philosophy, would necessarily include an awareness of the givens of existence, as well as intent to explore and clarify the particular experiences of the client. As ontic and ontological dimensions themselves reflect the general and the particular aspects of the human situation, respectively, these categories would both be referenced in any therapeutic exploration.

How a practitioner participates in the relationship with the client is probably the area in which there is the most variation among therapists. Some therapists feel it is their function to educate or direct their clients to 'better' ways of living and relating (seeing themselves as 'less clumsy at living' (Deurzen, 2008, p43)); others are more concerned that the client discovers for themselves what values they are choosing to live by, and how these are manifested in their lives (viewing themselves as fellow travellers).

Therapists also vary greatly in how 'personal' they are with their clients: some prefer the distance that allows for an existential analysis of the client's situation; others will use the relationship between the client and therapist as an avenue of exploration of the assumptions and expectations with respect to relatedness. This latter type of engagement allows for more disclosure and exposure on the part of the therapist: this is seen as an opportunity to reflect on the immediate relationship, and compare it to relationships external to the therapeutic encounter.

Cooper (2003, p144) charts the dimensions of existential approaches to therapy, and locates models and practitioners along the continuums between: phenomenological or existential; non-directive or directive; descriptive or explanatory; psychological or philosophical; individualising or universalising; pathologising or de-pathologising; subjective or inter-worldly; immediacy or non-immediacy; spontaneity or techniques.

Although some of these poles are diametrically opposed, others might be amalgamated under one paradigm: the most obvious of these is phenomenological and existential, where both foci would warrant attention in any existential therapy endeavour. It is also possible (and acknowledged by Cooper) that a therapist might feel that more spontaneity is appropriate with certain clients, and less so with others. This more variable stance reflects the fact that we are always situated in a context and in a relationship: we may respond to these aspects in different ways at different times.

What is important is that the practitioner works in a manner that is congruent with their own perspectives on their role in the therapeutic endeavour; this is something that should be subject to frequent review and reflection. The existential practitioner is likely to appreciate the human situation in terms of the descriptions offered in the literature, but they must meet every client, indeed every person, with an attitude of naïveté and generous curiosity.

71

ADOPTING AN EXISTENTIAL ATTITUDE

Everything is existential. There is no concern, choice, action or behaviour that cannot be understood with reference to the givens of existence: they are always an evasion of, response to and/or acknowledgement of these very human conditions.

The existential attitude is not an applied theory: it is a way of understanding how human beings exist in the world, bearing in mind that it is human beings who raise the question of their being, who recognise that there is no necessity to existence. It is also a way of living in recognition of, or even despite of, the universals of our existence.

The philosophers that are described as 'existential', even if this assignment is not applied to all their works, are those that explore and reflect on living. Nietzsche, Kierkegaard, Sartre, Heidegger, Merleau-Ponty, Buber and Tillich, to name a few, used their own lives to understand the world around them: their weaknesses, reflections, failures, faults, successes and relationships were all material for a deeper appreciation of what it means to be human. An understanding of the tenets of philosophers such as these encourages the existential practitioner to live a reflective life, and practice reflective psychotherapy. It is this very capacity to reflect that allows both client and therapist's self-construct to emerge and ultimately enables each of us to respond, adapt, flex and accept what we encounter. The existential therapist must have their own consistent framework with which to reflect on their lives and organise their experience if they are to assist their clients in finding a framework of their own (Deurzen, 2002). Only if they demonstrate an ability to live a deeply meaningful life, despite the apparent chaos and absurdity of human existence, can they hope to help their clients find ways to do the same.

The contributions of phenomenology to therapeutic practice (especially the offerings of Sartre and Heidegger) focus on a recognition that our awareness has a dynamic quality: therefore, our knowledge is limited, and our worldview is pliable, even if we do not wish it to be so. This promotes a humility in the existential therapist that precludes dogmatism, and an appreciation that everyone is subject to the same constraints. Accordingly, existential therapists are likely to have a perspective on the human condition that is broad and expansive, free from rigid conventions or ideologies (including therapeutic ones) and devoid of any interest in influencing or converting the client to their worldview. As Deurzen (2002, p27) states, 'the practitioner's message to their clients is to think for themselves'.

The existential attitude is not an intellectual exercise or a cognitive model; it is a way of comprehending life. The important thing for both therapist and client is to *be* existential (May *et al.*, 1958).

72

DESCRIPTIVE INTERPRETATION RATHER THAN EXPLANATION

Our perception of reality is a consequence of interpretation: it would be antithetical, then, to suggest that existential phenomenological practitioners do not make interpretations. It is more useful to consider what *kind* of interpretation is relevant in existential therapeutic work.

Heidegger demonstrates hermeneutic enquiry in *Being and Time*, offering us a 'spiral' interpretation of being, discussed in various stages. Each time he approaches the subject from a slightly different angle, and the understanding unfolds, and deepens. He begins with a general account of human existence, which he then refines, reconsiders and reinterprets (Polt, 1999). This exemplifies the quality of interpretation offered by the therapist: it is a tentative understanding, one that is dynamic, mutable and open to reinterpretation indefinitely. The understanding is current, but never complete.

As opposed to explanation, interpretation is not a conclusion: it is an understanding that awaits further understanding. If the therapist, having been able to understand the worldview of the client to some extent, offers an interpretation of a situation or a concern expressed by the client, it is only effective in so far as it resonates, or fails to resonate, with the client's understanding at that particular moment in time.

The interpretation offered by the therapist is in reference to the manifest material presented by the client: the meanings and values expressed in the communication are what is relevant to the client's worldview. The existential therapist doesn't apply theoretical suppositions to their interpretations. Instead, it is their curious and open stance to the client's understanding that grants credibility to any interpretations they might offer. Cannon (1991, p18) proposes, in fact, that the client and therapist are in 'partnership... in the mutual project of exploring and naming' the various aspects of the client's existence.

The focus on lived experience doesn't preclude an exploration of how the current understanding might apply to any number of situations in the client's life and world: the meanings may be subject to modification depending on context. The investigation of how and why this might be can yield further illumination of the assumptions, values and tensions inherent in the client's worldview.

In a hermeneutic interpretation, the lived experience of the client, whether current or historical, remains at the centre of the investigation: in this sense, the therapist is not detached from the interpretation, but is a participant in the process. There is no hidden significance; the many possibilities of meaning continue to extend and unfold in the process of reflection. The naïve curiosity of the therapist allows them to offer hypotheses and interpretations that refer to the client's previous descriptions of the assumptions and expectations. This dance of discovery can continue indefinitely.

73

BEING-WITH AND BEING-FOR THE CLIENT

Being-with-others is a condition of human existence: how this relatedness unfolds can be a source of joy, sorrow or any other experience along that continuum. Additionally, the quality of any relationship is changeable and ambivalent: we love, then we hate, then we feel both simultaneously, for example.

The emphasis on 'being' in the therapeutic relationship liberates the existential practitioner from prescribed modes of relating. They need not be warm, encouraging, congruent, supportive, etc., merely because this is what is expected of them in the role of therapist. Rather, they can respond to the client they meet, and the client is then free to respond to them: it is an essential part of the work that the therapist discover, in the client's interests, how this engagement is similar and different to those she has external to the therapeutic relationship.

Spinelli (2007) suggests two fundamental modes of being-with the client: 'being-with' and 'being-for'. These modes are mutually inclusive, and reflect the intentions to enter, and at least partially appreciate, the client's worldview.

'Being-with' the client is a stance that seeks to stay with the expressions of the client's experienced truths; this excludes any intentions on the part of the therapist to confirm, agree or disagree, or contradict. The exploration focuses on the meanings and values (implicit and explicit) expressed in the narrative: this will allow the revelation and appreciation of the client's 'worlding' (Spinelli, 2007): that is, their worldview as it is currently expressed in the therapeutic context.

In 'being-for' the client, the therapist foregoes, at least in the first instance, any notion of changing or judging the client's perspective, or of even 'helping' the client, as this would imply that the therapist knows what might be 'helpful'. Instead they seek to embrace the views, attitudes, assumptions and values that the client is expressing as valid and true for the client. They attempt to understand, and to some extent share, the client's horizon: to view the world and all the inter-relational components therein from the client's point of view, and to let it 'be'.

Acceptance such as this is not the same as agreement or validation: it is an apprehension that could be described as visceral, rather than intellectual; it is a deeply felt inter-subjective contact. A client whose values and behaviours are radically different from those of the therapist can still expect to experience acceptance from the therapist.

Such a reception allows the client to consider how they 'find' themselves in this encounter: how their expectations and assumptions about self, other and self-in-relation are being expressed, and in what ways these are true, partially valid or in need of review. This process occurs in the immediacy of the therapeutic engagement and is possible only because the therapist is able to sit with the client in the way described above.

The therapist is not immune to the impact of sharing an other's perspective at this level and can be affected as deeply, and in many of the same ways as the client: both recognise that they are experiencing an other, and have to consider what this might mean for their own assumptions about self, other and self-in-relation.

Being-with and being-for the client are not necessarily chronological or linear stages of therapy: they are modes of being-with that can serve the therapeutic endeavour at any juncture.

74

TAKING THE ROLE OF THE OTHER

We can never fully be fused with another human being, nor can we ever be totally isolated from all humanity: we exist on the continuum between these poles. The otherness of the therapist is reflected in their inability to totally share in the perspective of the client. This is not a failure on anyone's part: it is an impossibility with significant implications – it means that each of us is unique, but inevitably connected and related.

The existential therapist places an emphasis on a quality of being-with over 'doing' techniques in therapy. This grants a more genuine relationship, as it is a response to the specific client and the unique situation that the occasion provides. It also fosters a stance that supports an acceptance of the client's perspectives, and abjures the attempt by the therapist to correct or contest them according to a theoretical system. As a result a trust is created between the practitioner and the client that liberates the latter from having to defend or explain their position; the client is then more likely to take a more reflective view on their own assumptions. This is all in aid of a more adequate appreciation of the client's worldview, for both parties.

However, as suggested, the therapist will harbour their own biases and interpretations: these are sometimes bracketed in an effort to more clearly receive the client's position without imposing their own views. Once the perspectives of the client are understood to some extent, and the relationship between therapist and client has been grounded in trust, the therapist is then in a position to offer their own understanding of the client's worldview based on the disclosures of the client. Inevitably, this communication will have an interpretive quality, as it is sourced in an understanding emanating from the therapist who holds their own view on the world and its contents.

The therapist's response to the client's material will inevitably reflect their otherness: everything heard or perceived is interpreted. When appropriate, the therapist can offer their perspective on the client's situation: this would be with respect to how the client's worldview, in all its manifestations, is both a problem and a solution for the client. In this manner, the therapist demonstrates inclusion (Spinelli, 2007; Buber, 2013): the quality of the resulting encounter is a consequence of this inter-subjectivity.

The therapist does not have an 'objective' view on the client, but rather an inter-subjective one: the quality of the relationship emerges from the participation and contributions of both parties: how this has developed, how each person views their own involvement. It can be an opportunity for the client to discover and acknowledge the validity of another person's perception of them, as well as to appreciate that it might not match up with what they wish or expect. It can also be an opportunity to recognise how our views of self and other may change, according to how we understand and perceive the other.

Other aspects of the worldview can be reviewed, as these will all be implicated: self, other, world and cosmos constructs can be explored with respect to the presenting problem. If there are discrepancies or contradictions between or among the constructs, the implications for maintaining or modifying the assumptions and beliefs held in the worldview can be discussed; if one element is changed, the way this will affect other aspects can be explored. As Spinelli (2007, p148) points out, these investigations 'more adequately place the client's presenting problem in relation to the worldview'.

75

CHALLENGING WITH CURIOSITY AND DIRECTNESS

An existential therapist will be challenging rather than contesting. Challenging is quite different than contesting: the former is 'inclusive' – sourced in the expressions of the client that demonstrate their worldview – and includes the therapist's limited understanding of the client's perspective. A challenge that directly references a client's communications will hold more credibility and more possibility in terms of its effectiveness. Contesting, on the other hand, comes from a place where it is assumed the therapist is an expert, or holder of truth, about the client's situation.

Directness describes interactions that are immediate and frank. Directness is usually spontaneous and reflects the current situation, although it may also be in response to a previous event or discussion. Candour does not preclude diplomacy on the part of the therapist: thoughtfulness is always appreciated and helps contribute to the trust between both parties.

These communications emerge from a generous curiosity about and for the client: they are not theory-lead presumptions, but hypotheses and musings that are consequences of reflection and exploration of the client's experiences.

Challenges can be framed as summaries, reflections or paraphrases. Questions are less of a feature of existential therapy as they too often demand justification and can be experienced by the client as aggressive and judgemental.

The purpose of a challenge should never be to make the client wrong, but rather to open up a line of enquiry and reflection. For example, the therapist may respond to the client who declares that they are just not coping by asking them to reflect on ways in which they are and are not coping at that very moment.

If the client experiences the therapist as critical, and has the courage to disclose this, it can be an opportunity to reflect on the unfolding relationship between them. The therapist will maintain a stance of naïveté and curiosity, as they appreciate that their understanding of the client is situated and incomplete. This appreciation allows the therapist to 'hold' the client's feelings towards them in a way that enables them to be freely considered and explored.

The better a person feels understood and accepted, the more likely they are to trust the listener. However, if this trust is undermined, this too can be seen as an opportunity to reflect on and explore the assumptions and attitudes around this very fundamental relational condition. Such an opportunity is likely to occur in every therapeutic encounter at least once; it is almost inevitable that we will fail our clients in some way, unintentionally. This can be deeply disturbing and challenging for both of those involved: it is likely to be something that has resonance with events in relationships external to the therapy context. It may be unusual in that the breach becomes an event that is discussed openly, and possibly becomes the basis for a recovered trust. This, in turn, models a basis for the repair of breaches in trust outside of the therapeutic setting.

76

ASSUMING A DIALOGICAL ATTITUDE

The dialogical attitude indicates a willingness to enter a relationship of a particularly 'truthful' quality: it cultivates an appreciation for the implicit truths of those involved. Such an intention is more likely to succeed in an encounter that avoids systematic investigation, but fosters a creative exploration that is immediate and unpredictable. Spinelli (2007) makes clear that this is not a technique or an application, but an attempt to realise a particular quality of being with others.

This attitude results in a different kind of verbal exchange: dialogue differs from conversation in that it is less controlled or directed; the direction is created, not pre-determined. Therefore anything the client offers for discussion will somehow be appropriate: it is the nature of dialogue that the relevance is discovered. Existential therapists don't structure their client sessions in any particular way, nor do they look to create a continuation of a previous session by bringing up what they judged to be the key points raised in that session.

Dialogical communication is direct, but not directive: it is in the nature of a true exploration, where there may be diversions and dead-ends, and where the route is sometimes circuitous. In this quality of connection, confusion and even chaos, a position holding many possibilities is created – an expanse of themes and concerns. The client is encouraged to resist any attempt to make sense of this chaos, and to focus on description, allowing the full narrative to emerge unhindered by theories of causation.

Martin Buber (2013) is renowned for his treatise on dialogue as it occurs in an 'I–Thou' relationship. In this mode of being-with, each of those participating is wholly present to the other as an 'I' and at the same time as 'Thou'. Leslie Farber, commenting on Buber's work, states that 'truth is ... conceived in, and discovered in, dialogue' (Farber, 2000, p62). Farber goes on to propose that this encounter is available to anyone who can 'speak and listen'. Deurzen-Smith (1997) describes this mode as 'communion', a connection beyond communication.

Buber makes it clear that we cannot summon this quality of relating: we can only be available for it. Once again, the existential therapist is eschewing techniques in favour of taking a philosophical and reflective stance towards relating to the client.

This kind of relationship is deeply affecting for both participants, who cannot help but understand themselves, and the other, in a novel way. Such mutuality has its liabilities as well as benefits: both therapist and client must be willing to be affected, and to be open to the possibility of having their worldview challenged. Not every client (nor indeed every therapist) will be able to summon the courage to be open to such a challenge.

A dialogic encounter is episodic: it cannot be sustained, and perhaps should not be, as its impact needs to be processed and integrated. An existential therapist taking a dialogical attitude is merely acknowledging the possibility of such an encounter.

77

NORMALISING VERSES DIAGNOSING: AN EXISTENTIAL PERSPECTIVE

Diagnostics are a conclusion and an explanation: but an explanation is not the same as understanding, and a conclusion too often pre-empts further exploration. R.D. Laing suggested that the assignment of a diagnosis like schizophrenia was in fact a way of *not* understanding the person so classified (Laing, 1969). After all, such a label immediately creates in the therapist an expectation that the client will exhibit certain symptoms and behave in particular ways. It also comes with a ready-made explanation of the client's behaviour (they are behaving this way because they have an illness) and associated treatment protocols and prognoses.

Diagnosis of a pathology results in an objectification of existence, and 'makes it an impersonal something' (Binswanger, 1963, p102). It sources the understanding of a client in the opinion of an 'objective' professional, thereby minimising the opportunity for the individual who is objectified to participate in how they are understood. Such an intention or a result is antithetical to the deeply personal engagement espoused in existential phenomenological philosophy and psychotherapy.

Rollo May (1969) proposes that psychological diagnostics have their place: they are not the same as therapy; do not have the same functions; and are most often readily forgotten once the therapy has begun. The patient's problems have to be reformulated in light of their way of being-in-the-world.

This perspective has some credibility. It may be that diagnostics have a place, particularly in medical contexts. However, when one person labels or objectifies another, something happens to both of them, and between them. The relationship is relegated to a contact, not a connection, between 'objects'; what Buber might describe as an 'I–It' encounter, with little hope of much more.

What, then, might be considered 'normal'? In terms of psychiatry and models of psychopathology, this is another culturally and politically sourced term: if our behaviour is agreeable by consensus, then we are considered sane or normal (Laing, 1967).

Existential therapists resist seeing clients' feelings, behaviours, values or worldviews as normal or abnormal, accepting that there is no such thing as normality in an inherent sense – only socially constructed normality. Often the clients' fear of being 'not normal' causes as much or greater distress than the behaviour or feeling the label is attached to. Helping such clients to see that their worldview and everything they say, feel or do takes place in a context, and can be explained, reduces this fear.

For the existential therapist, what are referred to as 'disturbances' or 'symptoms' reveal ontological or 'being-related' issues (Cohn, 2002; Spinelli, 2007). These difficulties are sourced in concerns that are relevant to us all: personally and philosophically relevant, but also socially, morally and politically. It follows, then, that 'the symptomatic … behaviour of individuals differs only in degree – not in kind – from that of the "abnormal" individual' (Spinelli, 1989, p138).

All distress and disturbance is a manifestation of our responses to the givens of existence, including the inevitability of anxiety and suffering. The therapist hopes for a shared understanding of how the client is situated with respect to these conditions, even if this understanding is only partial. The removal of symptoms is not the aim: the discomforts are indicators of what needs to be acknowledged and addressed, and offer the client benefits of some kind that must be discerned, and alternative sources identified and chosen, if the 'symptom' is to be given up.

The assumptions, beliefs and expectations that comprise the client's worldview serve to allow them to function with some efficacy in the face of anxiety, guilt, mortality, responsibility and finitude. It may become evident that these strategies are more burdensome than the challenges they are meant to help them deal with. In this way, we are all subject to the same trials.

78

WORKING EXISTENTIALLY IN A TIME-LIMITED WAY

Time is a fundamental issue in existential literature. Heidegger's seminal work, *Being and Time*, contextualises all human existence with reference to time: death, finitude, anxiety, uncertainty and guilt – all the givens of existence are related to this phenomenon.

Existential psychotherapy, therefore, is a time-sensitive practice. However, all therapeutic models, and all human situations, are fundamentally time-limited in that they all come to an end.

In a practical sense, therapy has time boundaries: the sessions are agreed for a specific duration, the frequency of the sessions is decided and, very often, the number of sessions is specifically contracted. It is this latter aspect that seems to cause the most concern, especially when the number of sessions is deemed 'short-term' therapy.

Strasser and Strasser (1997) point out that the moment a time-limited therapeutic relationship is agreed, the way in which the therapist interacts with the client, the type of questions that will be asked and the goals and aims that will be set are changed.

We all experience time differently, in different contexts. Sometimes an hour passes too quickly, other times it feels interminable – how we experience any temporal framework is a matter of perception and interpretation. Therefore, to qualify a situation as 'short-term' is a demonstration of the attitude of the person making this evaluation: it is likely to be directly related to the expectations and aims of that individual.

As time is a given of existence, the manner in which the client, and the therapist, engage with this element is ripe for exploration: a clearly delineated time boundary can often focus the assumptions and expectations of both parties with respect to this aspect of life.

Whether the therapy contract is for weeks, months or years, it can be useful for the therapist and client to talk about how this boundary is experienced, and how this experience is representative, or not, of the client's life outside the therapeutic context. A client who feels demotivated by the limitations of an eight-session contract and considers not starting the work in light of this limitation might see a similar pattern in the way they approach projects in their everyday life.

A time-limited contract, as opposed to an 'open-ended' arrangement (which, in fact, does not exist), can specify a definitive ending, with no possibility for renewal or extension, or it may include a 'soft' ending, in which further time-limited modules may be agreed. In either case, it is most effective to make these boundaries explicit, in the same manner as the session duration is specified. This strategy promotes a consideration by all those involved of the attitudes to the time allotted, in therapy and in life.

Even though the time commitment may be agreed, there is no guarantee that either party will be able, or willing, to abide by the arrangement: each is free to change their mind, and each is subject to the contingencies of existence that may prevent the fulfilment of intentions. These are precisely the kinds of issues that time constraints can provoke: how to choose whether to 'spend' or 'keep' time; the nature of commitment in terms of time and others; the success and/or failure to realise ambitions and aspirations 'in time'; the implications of finitude.

Life rarely allows us 'enough' time: in a time-limited frame therapy, this concern is immediately in the forefront of the discussion between therapist and client. The existential therapist sees this constraint as more than just a contractual reality. It is in fact central to the therapy, with the potential to reveal much about the client's way of being-in-the-world. In time-limited therapy, time (as it is experienced and used by the client) becomes a tool (Strasser & Strasser, 1997).

79

USING MYTH, METAPHOR AND PHILOSOPHY

As Savery (2013) points out, sometimes words alone are 'insufficient symbols' for clients to express what it means to be human in all its twists and turns. On these occasions, myths – the stories that illustrate a cultural, religious or personal ideology – are useful narratives for the therapeutic context. Any story that has meaning for a client is an interesting and dramatic entry point for the exploration of what makes the fable meaningful, and how it reflects the worldview of the client. Myths, more often than not, hold relevance for particular social settings, and can assist in the discovery of the client's worldview with respect to this particular realm of existence.

Metaphor is a figure of speech that attempts to describe or define an experience, object or person by comparison to another: the similarities and distinctions in such an attribution can be discussed and considered by client and therapist. Metaphors can be selected from standardised representations – for example, 'the heart of a lion' – or they can be created by the client. As these are often more implicit than explicit comparisons, these too can be reviewed for the personal meanings they hold for the client. A client who says her childhood was 'like growing up in a refugee camp', for example, may, when prompted, describe the multicultural neighbourhood of her youth, with people of all colours and creeds popping in and out of her home. Alternatively, she may talk about uncertainty around the availability of food and a reliance on grandparents dropping by with 'food parcels'.

The therapist can introduce a myth or metaphor in the service of further elucidating the client's perspective. This can be effective, as long as the practitioner does not insist on its relevance – its usefulness can only be validated by the client.

When myth or metaphor are employed by the client in the course of their narrative, it shouldn't be regarded as a diversion or a distraction. The mythological character the client identifies with most or least in their story may provide a useful route to the perspectives the client holds on choice, relationship, freedom, responsibility, finitude and death. The tragedies and triumphs of any mythological tale always harbour a personal significance. Such symbolic representations of events, feelings or thoughts through myth and metaphor often allow the client to depersonalise their narrative enough to make the unbearable bearable and the unexplainable explainable.

Philosophy provides insight and understanding about the human condition. It can facilitate an appreciation of the issues and concerns that are entertained by many cultures, and across historical eras.

Existential philosophy does not offer a model for psychotherapy, but it can provide a perspective on existence. Philosophy is not applied in the usual sense – it is an attitude. The therapist's manner of engaging with the context of therapy, and the people involved in this enterprise, will be a reflection of their own worldview, that is, their assumptions and expectations of self, others, the world and the cosmos, their own particular philosophy of life.

If a therapist places a client issue or a part of the client's narrative within a philosophical context, it should be, again, in an effort to deepen the understanding of the client's view: it should not be delivered as a 'truth', but rather, in the spirit of any philosophical investigation, as a point for reflection and discussion. Tales like that of Sisyphus (Camus, 1942), for example, can be used to illustrate key existential themes such as meaningless and absurdity.

As myth, metaphor and philosophy all allude to common but dramatic situations in the affairs of human existence, they can provide a means of 're-introducing' the client to their own understanding of life and how they are living it.

80

EXPLORING SEXUALITY, GENDER AND IDENTITY IN EXISTENTIAL TERMS

There are few topics that provoke as much heated discussion as the role of 'nature' and 'nurture' as determinants of sexual identity, or indeed of identity in general.

Gender is slightly less problematic in that it is generally recognised as a socio-cultural characterisation: the definitions of genders vary with respect to historical, political and social contexts. As such, it is recognised as an assignment or an assumption of identity with more ambiguous attributes, and therefore more latitude for choice.

This text can't address the arguments pertinent to these themes in any depth; however, it is necessary to have some perspective on them in order to engage in an exploration of what might be therapeutic.

It is helpful to recall the proposal 'existence precedes essence'. With this pronouncement, Sartre is indicating that human beings are 'nothing' until they choose and act: in this way, we come into 'existence', as only human beings can.

When someone declares that they are 'a good person', or 'an alcoholic', or 'unlovable' or 'homosexual', they are in effect demonstrating an article of bad faith: they are seeking to objectively identify themselves as a 'something' that stands without freedom and responsibility.

The existential therapist doesn't aim to contest or attempt to 'correct' the report of the client: it is the task of therapy to explore the implications of the client's assumptions and to discover how these are manifest in all dimensions of their worldview. Pathologising terms such as 'sex addiction' or 'paraphilia' are avoided. The practitioner isn't concerned with what is normal/abnormal or if particular practices are moral or immoral. Instead, the focus is on exploring the client's experience of social approval/disapproval in relation to their practices.

From a phenomenological perspective, the client's review of their experiences of and attitudes towards these issues of identity are the areas that deserve attention: only by dialogic engagement with these will the client and therapist discover the ambiguities, contradictions or partial truths of the client's way of being-in-the-world.

It is important to understand how the client experiences themselves as subject to elements beyond their control or choice, as well as those contexts in which they may also acknowledge their agency.

We all occasionally experience some apprehension when we are not clear about what can be changed, and what lies beyond our influence: it is a dilemma commonly expressed in therapy, and in life. The answer to this query may be uncertain, but it requires an engagement with choice nonetheless: the options (both practical and attitudinal) that the client perceives to be available to them will likely be the basis for discussion.

As expressions and experiences of gender, sexuality and identity all have consequences in all relational realms (self-in-relation, the other-in-relation, self-being-in-relation-with-the-other), and in all dimensions of existence (the physical, the social, the personal and the spiritual), these are relevant avenues of exploration and reflection.

81

LEAPING AHEAD VERSUS LEAPING IN

'Leaping in' and 'leaping ahead' are concepts considered by Heidegger in both *Being and Time* (1962), and the *Zollikon Seminars* (1987). They are forms of being-with another, and refer to the manner in which we 'care' for someone else. Although these conditions refer to ontological modes, they bear relevance for the therapeutic encounter.

The most relevant quote comes from *Being and Time,* in which the author discusses possible conditions of relatedness: 'that which leaps in and dominates, and which leaps forth and liberates' (Heidegger, 1962, p159).

In the practice of psychotherapy, we may recognise that 'leaping in' represents those forms of intervention that appropriate the work that belongs to the client: making interpretations sourced in external contexts; making suggestions or giving advice; attempting to relieve the client of their responsibilities, for example. This latter activity is manifest in the desire on the part of the therapist to relieve the client of their suffering. By 'leaping in' in this way, the therapist deprives their client of the opportunity to discover their own resilience in dealing with difficulties, and assign their own meaning to life's struggles.

Such a strategy too often is in the service of the therapist who wishes to view themselves as a 'healer', mentor or tutor. It can be difficult to resist the desires of a client who wishes to be cured or corrected: the existential therapist recognises that they may need to sacrifice their own need for approbation to better serve their client.

Clients of therapists who leap in are less likely to be able to deal with any future challenges as they have experienced the resolution of their distress as something that was 'done to them' rather than something they effected themselves.

'Leaping ahead' or 'leaping forth' is a facilitative encounter: it encourages the client to engage with their situation in a way that is authentic and meaningful. It is, as Polt (1999) describes it, an 'unusual' phenomenon. In this mode of being-with, the therapist attends to the client in an effort to contribute to the clarification of what is true and meaningful for the client with respect to their worldview.

Ultimately, this is work that belongs to the client: we should eschew providing our own answers for, solutions to, or interpretations of the experiences and concerns of the people seeking our help. We travel alongside, not ahead of, our clients.

82

WISDOM AND THE PASSIONATE LIFE

Philosophy is a word derived from a Greek word meaning 'love of wisdom'. But defining wisdom can in itself be a daunting task: one person's wisdom is another's folly.

Such discrepancies between one person's perspective and another's indicate that wisdom is not necessarily about answers, or at least, answers that are acceptable to everyone. In his work *As You Like It*, Shakespeare (2012) went so far as to state that 'The fool doth think he is wise, but the wise man knows himself to be a fool'. Again, there is an implication that humility and a tentative approach to answers are indicators of wisdom.

What do we want for ourselves, for our loved ones, and for our clients? If we say 'to suffer less', we may exclude them from developing compassion for others; if we say 'a peaceful life', we may see them robbed of the development of resilience; if we propose the realisation of dreams, it is only through the struggle to make these dreams reality that they warrant value and success.

Friedrich Nietzsche called upon each of us to be 'artists of life' (Tanner, 1994): this is a call to the passionate life, a theme that resounds throughout his works. He advocates *more* life: more failures and successes, more trials and tribulations and greater appreciation of our weaknesses, and possibilities. Nietzsche deplored those who attempted to live by the values and morals handed to them: as existential therapists we can remind our clients that we have to wrestle with the how and why of living to create a very distinctive, very personal 'style' of living: our own style.

In creating this, our clients may suffer, as it is not an easy, or popular, effort. Such a stand challenges everyone else in our client's life too: are they living the life that is their own, or a second-hand version of how and what it *ought* to be?

But the pain is not wasted: 'Greatness ... involves putting pain to work' (Tanner, 1996, p27). We are called upon to do just that: not just to accommodate the pain, but to make it useful, if not 'beautiful'. This requires artistry, as suggested earlier. Our life becomes our art, our passion.

We often hear in our work with clients that they deplore their mistakes: they are immobilised by their imperfections, laden with regret. But the person who lives a passionate life, according to Nietzschean principles, is not concerned with so-called failures: the challenge is to rise to the opportunities for grace and re-creation that they introduce.

Our clients may need to acknowledge their grief, their losses: it is a part of life's process. But when their sorrows become their raison d'être, instead of the engagements with life's challenges, then we as therapists have the opportunity to observe and point out the further losses, and subsequent regrets that may be the consequences of a life without consummate involvement and passion.

83

WORKING EXISTENTIALLY WITH GROUPS

The existential phenomenological perspective proposes that human existence is fundamentally relational and inter-subjective. Even an attempted withdrawal from the relational context implies an ongoing connection, a stance taken to our relatedness: we cannot fully extricate ourselves from the 'with-world'. We may try to maintain our distance, but it remains that we must have something to distance ourselves from.

It follows from this that group psychotherapy could provide a therapeutic opportunity: in this context one and all might discover how they contribute to the quality of relationships, and how they affect, and are affected by, others in their wider external relational matrix. It can provide a greater inter-relational complexity (Spinelli, 2007), one that cannot be duplicated in individual therapy, although those inter-subjective factors would certainly be part of the exploration in any therapy.

An existential phenomenological approach to group work would be characterised by a few distinct factors. The most significant of these are noted by Cohn:

1 'The therapist does not "stand out" hierarchically "over against" others' (Cohn, 1997, p55)
2 'The group is the therapist of the group' (Cohn, 1997, p46)
3 There is no 'inside' or 'outside' with reference to appropriate narratives or material: whatever is brought to the group in terms of events or concerns that occur within the group or alternatively in the wider social contexts of the members' lives is given equal consideration.

Point 1 above suggests that the group therapist, or facilitator, is not granted any expertise or authority in terms of their input or perceptions. As they are one among others, they are at liberty to participate in much the same way as any of the members, and stand responsible for the effects of their contributions. The only difference in the role of the facilitator is that they outline the practicalities of the therapeutic contract.

Point 2 proposes that as the group develops, the members will become the facilitators of the therapeutic possibilities. They will be the explorers, the interpreters, and the reflective participants of their experiences of themselves-in-relation, both within and outside of the group itself.

This latter proposal also covers the principle described in Point 3. This indicates that there will be some occasion for group members to consider how their experiences within the group both replicate and differ from how they engage with the external and extensive networks of which they are part, and the significance of these similarities and discrepancies.

Corey (2009) describes the goals of existential group therapy as being focused around broadening members' perspectives of themselves and the world around them, facilitating their efforts to be honest with themselves and helping them discern what gives meaning to their lives. Cohn suggests that the opportunity to reflect on and review the strategies and assumptions held in reference to how we relate is best served by the group experience: 'therapy … is a process that takes place between people' (Cohn, 1997, p51).

84

EXISTENTIAL RELATIONSHIP THERAPY

Paradoxically, although existential philosophy recognises the centrality of relationship to human existence, until recently very little was written about how this translated into practice in relationship therapy. As Deurzen and Iacovou (2013, p239) state, existential therapists:

> are uniquely placed to work with clients who are confused, disillusioned and dismayed by the challenges and demands that come from 'being-in-the-world-with-others' (Heidegger, 2003).

The theoretical underpinnings of a model of existential relationship therapy are the same as those for individual therapy. Indeed, the existential therapist would argue that *all* therapy is relationship therapy – for even if the client attends alone, the primordial nature of relatedness in human existence is addressed both in discussions of the client's relationships outside of the therapeutic space but also in the active use of the relationship within the room as a therapeutic tool.

Existential therapists encourage clients to recognise the freedom, choice and responsibility they have within their relationships. In order to achieve intimacy with others, we need to abandon the 'twin pitfalls of bad faith' (Deurzen & Iacovou, 2013, p232) – an overemphasis on facticity (a conviction we can't control anything in our relationships) and an overemphasis on freedom (a conviction we can control everything in our relationships) – and be truly open to the 'otherness' of our partner.

Leontiev (2013, p235) points out the inevitably of conflict in relationships when he says 'The Other is across the border of Me'. Existential therapy doesn't aim for harmony, therefore, but rather for an ongoing engagement with challenge and disagreement in the hope that mutual respect and understanding will emerge. This aim is achieved through the development of shared meaning and purpose in the relationship or, on some occasions, through an appreciation that shared meaning is not possible.

Existential relationship therapy offers clients the chance to uncover the 'sedimented beliefs' (Spinelli, 2007) that block their growth, intimacy and connectedness with others. In doing so, it is hoped that clients will identify new possibilities for their ways of being in relation and will recognise the potential inherent in these possibilities.

Existential therapists need to demonstrate personal strength, courage and connectedness in order to encourage the same in their clients. They should be willing to challenge clients who are acting in bad faith, or attempting to avoid the dilemmas of relatedness, while also retaining a sense of humour and playfulness when listening to their stories.

Not all clients will flourish in a therapeutic setting where responsibility, authenticity and willingness to respond to challenge are central to the process. Therefore it is important that the existential therapist shares the basic assumptions behind her work with clients at an early stage. The clients who will best benefit from existential relationship therapy are those who have both an ability and a willingness to explore and confront their worldviews and the component values, beliefs and ideas from which they are constructed. Of course, these skills can be developed over the course of the therapy. It is only if 'individuals continuously obstruct that process and persist with negativity or unwillingness to consider their own attitude that the therapeutic work may be judged to be impossible' (Deurzen & Iacovou, 2013, p238).

Part 4

ETHICS AND EXISTENTIAL THERAPY

85

CHOOSING WHO TO WORK WITH

It is both the therapist and the client who choose who to work with. In an initial consultation, it is useful to be explicit about this arrangement: both parties are responsible for making the kind of enquiries that would, at least at this juncture, satisfy them as to whether this alliance is workable or not.

Even when working with an organisation that provides or refers clients, this choice is extended to all those involved. In those rare instances in which a client is forced by some official body to attend therapy, the practitioner has an ethical responsibility to ascertain whether it is they in particular that can offer the best service for the client.

Unlike other models of therapy, the existential practitioner is not likely to use 'objective' criteria by which to decide whether a client is suitable for the work. The exception to this would be a client who has expectations of *treatment,* in the more common sense: existential practitioners do not *treat* symptoms; they *meet* people in distress, or with problems in living.

Deurzen (2002) points out that clients can only benefit from the existential approach in so far as they feel able to go along with its basic assumptions. It might be more relevant, therefore, to consider in what way a client might not be satisfied with what is on offer. If a client expects, for example, transference interpretations, the therapist might indicate that this technical term is not relevant to their own outlook, but that the relationship between themselves and the client is always available for discussion. Such a 'reframing' is not meant to mislead the client, but can serve as a starting point for considering what is needed, or expected.

If a client insists on a *treatment model* – say, for a specific behaviour, like fear of flying – the existential therapist would find it ethically necessary to clarify that this kind of programme is not on offer. The therapist must have a simple, brief and clear explanation of what they see as the aims of the work; however, it is more useful usually to listen carefully to what the client is looking for, and then respond specifically to their concerns.

It is in the meeting with another that our more subjective perspectives are in play. We may be aware of how we respond to each other, how we 'feel' our way through this first encounter, and how the other indicates their experience of the engagement as well.

It is not necessary to *like* a client; and likewise it may not be necessary for the client to *like* the therapist for there to be a sound basis for the work. What seems to be more important is a minimal amount of trust that the other, whether client or therapist, will be safe enough to engage in a relationship. Safety can mean any number of things in any given situation: physical safety is, of course, the fundamental necessity, but safety more often refers to a mutual respect for the other's perspective: this does not preclude disagreement, but it does disallow intentional threat to another's wellbeing, in any form.

Being a 'qualified' practitioner does not endow us with psychic powers: we cannot totally appreciate the other person's intent. These human relationships are subject to any and all of the possibilities, for better or worse, that are present in any human contact. A large degree of uncertainty is to be expected when making decisions as to the advisability of entering into or continuing a relationship.

86

CONFIDENTIALITY, NOTE-TAKING AND RELATIONS WITH OUTSIDE AGENCIES

Note-taking is often a requirement demanded by accrediting or registering bodies. However, whatever latitude exists within or external to these obligations leaves scope to consider what to write, as well as whether and how these notes are useful. There is also significant concern as to the privacy of such records, especially in organisational settings.

If notes are kept, the client's identity must be kept confidential: the records may reflect elements of the work, and the processes that are observed or experienced by those parties involved, but specifics that would identify the person seeking therapy must be avoided. Usually, this privilege of confidentiality does not extend to the practitioner. The therapist should also consider whether to tell the client that they do or do not keep notes: a consequence may be that the client wishes to read the records, which poses yet another ethical and practical dilemma for the practitioner. There are circumstances in which access to client records can be requested and so it is advisable to write notes with this in mind. These parameters must be observed in the production of case studies, whether or not they appear in published form.

Confidentiality is paramount in the establishment of trust. The extent of this aspect of the contract should be made explicit, as both the law and ethical considerations may impose limitations to what can be kept private. Both clear contracting and confidentiality foster trust in the therapist and the process: there should be no surprises, although, of course, not every contingency can possibly be covered.

If it is necessary to breach confidentiality, codes of professional practice usually stipulate that the client should be informed of the intention, and whenever possible, included in the means of disclosure.

Contact with external agencies is most often a consideration when working under the aegis of an organisation: most of these agencies will have some policy in place to address what is a common issue. If the therapist is at liberty to make this decision independently, it is preferable that this request originate with the client. If, after joint discussion with the client, the two agree such a disclosure, it is best that they collaborate on a written record that specifically states that it has been composed and submitted with the knowledge and participation of the client. Such communication with external sources should be carefully considered with respect to the wellbeing of the client.

The therapist should recognise that any non-observance of confidentiality puts the practitioner, as well as the process of therapy, at risk. It is therefore strongly suggested that this issue, should it arise, be discussed in the therapy and in supervision.

Finally, it should be pointed out that the existential therapist would not ordinarily make use of notes between sessions – to help prepare for future meetings, for example. This is because each session begins anew, with the client and therapist in the here and now. What was relevant or top priority in previous sessions may now be irrelevant or unimportant. The right of the client to direct their own therapy takes precedence over any need the therapist might have to create continuity or take control over the topics for discussion.

87

ASSESSING AND MANAGING RISK

When a client expresses the intention to self-harm, or states that they are already self-harming, it can present quite a challenge to practitioners.

Although the therapist cannot really prepare for the effect such a disclosure may have on them, they can consider their own perspectives on self-harm, and the ultimate prerogative of suicide on the part of the client. This reflection should take place in advance of engaging in therapeutic work, and the therapist's position reviewed regularly in light of their experience and development and in conjunction with professional mandates and legal requirements.

The most commonly acknowledged ethical positions are that both life and the wellbeing of any human being is the foremost consideration, or alternatively, that the individual's autonomy takes precedence over any value that might impede their agency. Regardless of the stance taken by the therapist, assessing the risk inherent in the behavioural strategies of any client is an inherent part of the therapeutic process. The consideration of whether and how to make a practical intervention is the more awkward decision for the therapist. The consequences of this choice must be carefully considered and shared in supervision, and it is generally regarded as good practice to include the client in a discussion of practicalities. It is important to have clear contracting around such possibilities; however, boundaries and contracts rarely cover every contingency, and human relationships and dilemmas do not fit neatly into prescribed frameworks.

There are classic parameters for assessing risk pertaining to self-harm, particularly in cases where there is clear communication from the client that suicide is being entertained as a possibility. These include the frequency and duration of the ideas, the particulars of the plan or activities, the accessibility of the means being considered, and the extent to which the chosen method would be lethally effective. These considerations are likely to be useful in discussing any form of self-harm: behaviours that may not seem fatal may nonetheless yield serious consequences.

The exploration of the client's values and how they are manifested in their worldview will reveal the choices and resulting behaviours of the client: how or to what extent these behaviours support their values will also emerge from these discussions. What most often comes to light in the case of self-harm or suicidal ideations is ambivalence about the choices available to the client.

Such an exploration can produce an agreement between the therapist and client as to how the situation might be 'managed': this will be based on how the problem is understood by both.

John Heaton, in his chapter on suicide and despair (Barnett 2008), proposes that such conditions are a way of 'existing'; this would indicate that the decision as to how both therapist and client engage with the difficulty will be specifically related to the client's way of being-in-the-world. Furthermore, as being-in-the-world always involves others, including the therapist, the implications for all individuals that might be impacted by the client's decisions should be considered openly. As Sartre (1943) asserts, when we choose, we choose not only for ourselves, but also for everyone else.

88

THE ISSUE OF POWER IN EXISTENTIAL THERAPY

Power does not exist independently of a context: it is always power over something or someone. The dynamic of power relates directly to the existential given of uncertainty in that we struggle with the contingencies of existence: it could all be otherwise, and our power to control such arbitrariness is limited. We may experience control over choosing an option, but we haven't the power to affect all the consequences of our choice – something that many clients struggle with, often becoming frozen in place at the realisation that they cannot predict every eventuality that might emerge from their actions.

As it is dynamic, power ebbs and flows. Only in very specific contexts are we in control, or are subject extensively to the power and control of another person. One person may seek power over another, even to the point of physical coercion, but they cannot exercise power over an individual's attitude.

Power is related to the existential aspect of freedom as well: our power over or against another may impede the other's freedom in a practical sense. One person may curtail another's practical options, as in the case of imprisonment. However, as noted previously, our perspective on any situation is where we can exercise the greatest extent of personal freedom. Frankl (2004) vividly describes this in the context of the Nazi concentration camps, when he reflects on the strength gained by those prisoners who chose to ascribe meaning and hope to their experiences.

On those occasions we feel we have power or control over our situation, we become all the more anxious to maintain this position: paradoxically, and simultaneously, we also sense our ultimate powerlessness to stabilise our control indefinitely.

These existential considerations bear implications for the therapeutic encounter: all that is possible in life is possible in therapy (although not all is desirable, as in life).

Spinelli (1994) disentangles many of the concerns related to imbalances and possible abuses of power in psychotherapy. With the support of other noteworthy writers and practitioners, he notes that power is owned by both therapist and client, in different ways, and at different times. The therapist may be in a position to set fees, and frequency and duration of the sessions, for example, but the client is at liberty to contest these, or to breach the particulars they once agreed upon. In more extreme circumstances, the client may inflict verbal, emotional or even physical abuse upon the therapist: these mutual potentialities may remain implicit, but they can serve to address imbalances that may be more obvious.

The possibilities for abuse and exploitation may be varied in terms of equality and sometimes common to both parties; but there are options available to either participant. It might be said that it is only in very rare circumstances, unlikely to occur in the therapeutic endeavour, in which power is absolute or exclusive to one individual.

However, Spinelli (1994) does advise that it is an ethical and moral obligation for the therapist to consider how the client might be experiencing the practitioner, and the process, as disempowering, exploitive or even abusive. He suggests that as the practitioner seeks to understand and challenge the worldview of the client, they too must be prepared to consider their own limited vision and subjective truths with respect to their theoretical assumptions. Herein, he notes, lie the most likely possibilities for the therapist's abuse of power: to insist on their own interpretation or understanding of the client's situation at the expense of the client's own.

89

SELF-DISCLOSURE IN AN EXISTENTIAL FRAMEWORK

Self-disclosure on the part of the therapist is one of the most frequent but least acknowledged interventions in therapeutic work. The kind of self-disclosure to be discussed here is an intentional and considered verbal communication.

The over-riding purpose in any intervention is to facilitate the client's clarification of their worldview, and how their choices are informed by their values and assumptions. It is useful to reflect on how the disclosure is in the service of the client: such a reflection would pre-empt comments that were delivered primarily to secure the comfort or authority of the practitioner.

The existential therapist does not assume a position of objectivity, but rather works from the standpoint of inter-subjectivity. They understand that their perceptions and those of their clients are subject to interpretations, and that such perceptions are directly related to the current inter-personal engagement, although perhaps not solely. It may be effective for the therapist to disclose, with candour, how they experience the two-in-relationship – but this should be offered tentatively and succinctly. This should be followed by an invitation to respond to the disclosure, and the reaction should be received without defence, as it is, at that juncture, true for the client.

Such a dialogue not only imparts information about perceptions and possible mis-perceptions, but also models a genuine encounter, with intent to assume a portion of the responsibility for the quality of the relationship.

It should be noted that honesty does not mean the communication of all concerns or perceptions: it is more effective to address the immediate question or encounter. Additionally, candour does not preclude the prerogative of privacy, on the part of both therapist and client. It is not likely or even necessary that everything will be revealed: it is enough that the work fulfils to some extent the aim of the therapeutic process.

With these principles in mind, it is usually more effective for the therapist to respond to questions put to them directly: the answer should be brief, and it may be that the therapist replies that they wish to consider the question, even for another session, before they reply. It is also possible that the practitioner may decide they do not wish to give an answer on the basis of privacy: such a communication is sound and reasonable, and indicates that the client owns the same option.

These kind of verbal exchanges are opportunities to explore the concerns related to direct questions from the client, as well as their response to any intentional disclosure from the therapist. These communications reflect the proposal that the relationship between the therapist and client is a genuine one, a specific encounter, although it may bear similarities to those in the client's wider social or familial contexts.

Finally, self-disclosure on the part of the therapist should be acknowledged as their own perception, and as a perspective that is available for review and re-interpretation. The practitioner may also take the opportunity both privately and in supervision to reflect on their own experience of these exchanges. After all, if the client the therapist meets in the room is the client that they meet in the room on that particular day (Cohn, 1997), then every therapeutic encounter brings the opportunity for a new stance on this (and other) therapeutic practice.

90

EXISTENTIAL SUPERVISION SKILLS

The skills for existential supervision reflect the idea that an existential perspective is an attitude for living in general; the work is more a *way of being* than applied techniques. Deurzen and Young (2009) describe existential supervision as something entirely different from traditional supervision (where the focus is on improving the supervisee's knowledge base or identifying the client's intra-psychic processes). In existential supervision 'we are involved in a process in which we formulate ideas, comment on the concerns of another and in doing refer to our own values, beliefs and ideas about life' (Deurzen & Young, 2009, p10).

The aim of existential supervision is closely aligned with that of existential therapy, that is, to explore the worldview of the client. It differs in that the worldview of the therapist is also considered with reference to how it might affect the process and the relationship.

Much of the work in supervision is around the convergence and divergence of perspectives between the therapist and the client: how does the therapist understand the client's position, and how is this impacted by the therapist's own bias? The discussion helps clarify what impedes the therapist's appreciation of the client's predicament, as well as the evidence provided in the reported dialogue that indicates that the client has indeed felt understood.

It is hoped that the therapist and supervisor will identify the existential issues implicated in the client's dilemmas, and how the client is engaging with these issues. Similarly, it is helpful if the supervision examines how the practitioner negotiates these themes, and how they are affected by the client's struggles. It can be an opportunity for the supervisor and therapist to review how the therapist contributes to the process and to the relationship, and to make explicit their hopes and expectations for any particular client.

Additionally, how the therapist relates to the supervisor can be illuminating in terms of the client work: for example, if the supervisee becomes defensive and balks at articulating the rationale for their work, the supervisor may suspect that the practitioner has not given enough thought to the intentions and aims of the therapy. Alternatively, if a supervisee is willing to consider other perspectives on their interventions and quality of engagement, with both their client and the supervisor, then it is likely that they will not be dogmatic or theory-led in their work.

Supervision shouldn't be about what is 'right' or 'wrong'; rather, it is an opportunity to reflect on how the communications and the quality of the therapist–client alliance serve to facilitate the clarification of the client's worldview. On occasions when the therapist feels they have failed their client, or have been distracted from their purpose, it can benefit both practitioner and client for the supervision to focus on the origins of the misguided intention, and how the therapist might work with the situation in the future.

Interventions qualified as 'mistakes' serve to demonstrate that all relationships are subject to misunderstandings, conflict and unintentional hurt – such events are unavoidable. What can be learned from such errors is that they are rarely fatal: rather, they can be opportunities for deepening the understanding between those involved, and serve to engender humility.

91

LIFE AFTER EXISTENTIAL THERAPY

All relationships end, one way or another, and therapy is no exception. The ending of therapy may be planned and carried out in a timely fashion, or it may end abruptly due to unforeseen developments or extreme circumstances.

The conclusion of therapy can often prompt a review of the work and how it has impacted on the life of both client and therapist. How the therapeutic work and engagement is evaluated may change over time, for both parties involved, as past experiences become interpreted in light of more current understandings.

Even before a practitioner begins a therapeutic engagement, they are likely to harbour some hopes and expectations of what the outcome may be, for themselves, as well as for their client. For existential practitioners, these ambitions on behalf of the client would include a greater tolerance and understanding, if not appreciation, of the challenges that face all of us: freedom and responsibility, temporality and finitude, relatedness, and uncertainty, to name a few. Additionally, our engagements with these givens can result in a wide variety of emotional experiences: joy, suffering, grief, satisfaction and anxiety, for example. These emotional experiences, it is hoped, will be understood as indicators of the values that comprise the worldview: the exploration and awareness of our worldview and how it informs our choices is a recognised goal of the therapeutic project (this can occur for the practitioner, as well as for the client). Even many of the difficulties too often described as 'pathological' may be understood in light of the assumptions and perspectives that underpin the worldview.

It is hoped that the client will exit with an understanding of the nature of philosophical enquiry: the clarification of the questions, rather than a slavish adherence to immutable answers. In the adoption of a naïve attitude, the existential therapist demonstrates that understanding is always limited, and that un-knowing presents greater opportunities for discovery and change. As Adams (2013) notes, many clients don't have much experience of what makes for a good ending, and it is hoped that the ending of existential therapy can be handled in such a way that it allows them to approach endings more effectively in the future.

Life after therapy has similar effects for the therapist as for the client: never again will either be exactly the same, as every other relationship will have qualities that will be particular to those specific encounters. Even if the two parties agree to consider meeting again professionally, this unique contact will be lost, given over to a particular time and place and situation. As with every relationship, the ending is an integral part of the engagement.

Part 5

BRINGING IT ALL TOGETHER

92

CRITICAL PERSPECTIVES ON EXISTENTIAL PSYCHOTHERAPY

As a philosophical enterprise, rather than a psychological or medical one, existential psychotherapy doesn't look for absolute answers: the issues of life that are the well-springs for both problems and satisfaction are not solvable. Embracing such a perspective can be difficult for clients: they generally wish to dispense with their suffering and discomfort.

This position can also be awkward for existential therapists: most would like to offer remedies for the distress endured by clients. However, practitioners do recognise that 'curing' human difficulties may also deprive clients of the insight that is possible in understanding their dilemmas, and also of the occasion to summon the courage that is necessary to live a meaningful life.

Additionally, precisely because it is a philosophical project, existential psychotherapy favours the subjective 'truth' to that of scientific 'objective' truth: this makes the approach less accessible to quantifying analysis. Generally speaking, existential practitioners describe their work as an 'approach' rather than a model: as an attitude that encompasses all aspects of one's life, not just therapeutic work. This can be problematic if what is sought is a measurable outcome that is tied to a specific methodology of practice.

It is a popular notion that existential philosophy and therapy focus on the more painful or uncomfortable aspects of life: death, suffering and guilt are topics that are frequently alluded to in this context. In his well-known work *The Ways of the Will and Other Essays* (2000), Leslie Farber deplores the morbid foci of the 'Thanotologists', and proposes that such an obsession with death, dying and suffering serves as a diversion from living life to the fullest. Such a criticism has some merit: a singular commitment to these aspects with little regard for other conditions could undermine a wider appreciation of all that human existence has to offer.

But what is overlooked in such an analysis is that we cannot refer to any one aspect of existence without implicating another. An exploration of any of life's conditions will necessarily reference another: such juxtapositions almost defy a singularity of focus.

There is no scientific, philosophical or psychological perspective on human existence that can satisfactorily or completely define the mystery that is life: life is a work in progress, carried out by beings that are complex and that operate in a world that is chaotic. Such a lack of certainty and permanence disallows solutions or remedies that are not themselves contingent and arbitrary.

The consequence of the philosophical enquiry that is the heart of existential philosophy and psychotherapy is a clarification of those questions that are significant for us: answers are viewed as positions that are subject to constant review and modification; life becomes an experiment. To embrace such a perspective may raise anxiety in the face of such impermanence, but it is a position of creativity, and the matrix for a display of courage and resoluteness.

93

A CRITIQUE OF THE DOMINANT SCIENTIFIC PARADIGM IN PSYCHOTHERAPY

A style of psychotherapy modelled on philosophical principles doesn't readily align itself with scientific paradigms.

Science certainly has a role: one would probably prefer a medical doctor to a philosopher (or psychotherapist) in submitting to a surgical procedure. However, when it comes to assigning meaning to an experience or a perception, many would chafe at the totalising and prescriptive description emerging from a scientific explanation. And to a large extent, therein lies the discrepancy between the two approaches: the philosophical is inclined towards understanding from a subjective or inter-subjective perspective, which implies limited truth and knowledge; the scientific is more focused on explanations that too often signal a definitive, 'objective' and 'value free' conclusion.

How is it, then, that scientific models are so pervasive in the field of explaining and treating human suffering and distress?

In his text *Trauma, Culture, Meaning and Philosophy*, Patrick Bracken (2002) traces the proclivity in Western culture for the scientific to Descartes' proposals. In his reasoning, Descartes proposes the soul as a *thing* that thinks: this objectifying of the spirit of humans has persisted. In conjunction with the Enlightenment, Descartes' proposals cleared the way for a popularisation of orientations in the human sciences based on empiricism, naturalism and positivism.

But why, we may ask ourselves; what is the appeal of this objectifying perspective?

In a scientific model, generally speaking, anything and everything can be measured. It can be quite comforting to adopt such an assured position of 'knowing': if things and people can be ultimately defined, then they harbour no surprises and are therefore less threatening.

What causes humans so much pain and discomfort is not knowing: not knowing what is the 'right' decision that will produce the precisely desired results; not knowing fully and finally who the other person is, and indeed, the same could be said for ourselves; not knowing when the winds of misfortune will descend upon any of us; not knowing if we can survive the challenges that will appear in spite of our best efforts to secure a peaceful life.

Empiricism and naturalism are views that embrace a theory of causality – the natural sciences have enjoyed much success on the basis of this methodology. From an existential perspective, such predicative power over the contingencies of human existence would be appealing. However, there is a price to pay for adopting the premises of scientific orientations as the basis for understanding the human condition: if we are products of mechanistic processes, then our agency is reduced to a delusion. In his book *Aping Mankind*, Tallis (2011, p51) warns that if we buy into contemporary scientific paradigms, like those he terms 'Darwinitis' and 'neuromania', then 'We may have to jettison the notion of freedom, and consequently, our personal responsibility .... Our destiny, like that of pebbles and waterfalls, is to be predestined'.

If these rather bleak, spiritless depictions of human existence were to any large extent credible, the need for and efficacy of all humanistic practices, including theology, philosophy and psychotherapy, would be rendered meaningless.

94

RESEARCH AND THE EFFECTIVENESS OF EXISTENTIAL THERAPY

Existential therapy doesn't lend itself to measurement, standardisation and manualisation – it cannot be *done to* a client but rather is *experienced with* the client. Therefore most research on the effectiveness of existential therapy has been qualitative rather than quantitative – focused on understanding the lived experiences of the client (and/or the therapist). Texts clarifying the methodologies and guiding principles of these research methods have long been available (see, for example, Manen, 1997; Smith, 2011); more recently, specific methodologies based on phenomenological-existential principles have emerged from psychology, including Interpretative Phenomenological Analysis (Smith *et al.*, 2009) and Descriptive Phenomenology (Giorgi, 1985).

A great deal of debate in psychotherapy research takes place around the use of randomised controlled trials (RCTs) – often said to be the 'gold standard' of research methods. As well as questioning whether it is possible or desirable to standardise any therapeutic approach (a pre-requisite for any RCT-based study), most existential therapists/researchers would argue that there are a number of fundamental flaws in the theory behind RCTs. First, and fundamentally, they require the drastic simplification of human experience into hypotheses, variables and outcomes that can be defined and then measured quantitatively. They also require an acceptance that research/the researcher can be objective and independent. Existential philosophy recognises that we are beings-in-the-world. We cannot stand apart from that world, and therefore any research we conduct will inevitably be influenced by our values, beliefs and assumptions. We can attempt to bracket our worldviews, but cannot escape them completely, and do better to acknowledge this in our research than claim that we can be dispassionate reporters of reality. Finally, RCTs on psychotherapy assume that certain symptom-related outcomes are inherently the most meaningful ways to measure the impact of the therapeutic process. Existential therapists see 'symptoms' as valid ways of being-in-the-world and do not have their reduction or eradication as a key aim of therapy.

Despite these concerns, existential therapists, like all therapists, are coming under increasing pressure to prove the effectiveness of their work and to do so in a form and language that health services and other funding bodies can understand. It is likely, therefore, that more attempts will be made to measure specific outcomes of existential therapy, such as the client's level of wellbeing, sense of meaning or ability to live a passionate life. Existential therapists will continue to vigorously debate the value of research that seeks to fragment the unique, complex and dynamic experience that is existential therapy in order to sell it to those who do not share its values or assumptions. However, most would accept that existential therapy, indeed all forms of therapy, should, to some extent at least, be 'research informed'. Existential therapy can never be 'research-directed', however, as research must take its place alongside philosophy, the therapist's and client's worldview and values, therapeutic theory, the therapist's experience and, of course, the lived moment between therapist and client, in determining how existential therapy should be conducted.

95

SHARED ORIGINS, MULTIPLE DIRECTIONS

There is a great deal of agreement with respect to many philosophical themes that inform the practice of existential therapy, and there is also an interesting divergence in the emphases on these themes and the resulting styles of working.

In his text on existential philosophy (1972), John Macquarrie suggests that as this 'style' of philosophising does not adhere to a central body of work(s), it is difficult to systemise precisely what defines existential thought. However, it is just this kind of systemisation that the recognised proponents of the philosophy eschew: human subjectivity, rather than objectivity, is the source for a philosophy of existence; the unique manner in which every person carries out their existence does not readily align with panrationalism, or positivism.

In a similar vein, existential psychotherapists may appreciate the themes that are central in understanding the human condition, but each therapist will themselves respond in their own way to the unique situation, and to the particular relationship that they encounter with every client, indeed, with every session.

In his comprehensive work, *Existential Therapies* (2003), Mick Cooper reviews the mainstream proponents of existential practice and delineates dimensions that have the greatest commonality across these styles. Cooper (2002, p145) refers to these dimensions as 'practice dilemmas'. Here, he compares recognised approaches and practitioners with respect to these dimensions. These foci include, among other things: individualising/universalising; immediacy/non-immediacy; subjective/inter-worldly. These are presented in the context of a continuum, and practitioners and approaches are notated with regard to where they might be placed on the scale in terms of style of working. This is a manageable overview of distinctions in practice.

In an attempt to describe the philosophical principles central to an existential phenomenological practice, garnered from a wide array of perspectives derived from existential material, Spinelli (2003) settles on three proposals that appear to be embraced by most practitioners: relatedness, uncertainty and existential anxiety. He goes on to elucidate these principles in some depth, and with reference to philosophical proposals. However, Spinelli (2003, p10) notes, 'there exist as many unique expressions of existential psychotherapy as there are unique beings who engage in it'.

It appears that there are some commonalities among existential therapists with reference to philosophical sources, and an innumerable amount of distinctions with respect to style of practice. These convergences and divergences reflect philosophical proposals that have been discussed in this text: as human beings, we all share common concerns, and as each of us has a unique perspective on the world, we each have a distinct way of engaging with these concerns.

Just what might be described as 'existential' practice remains a constant source of discussion and debate, but it is unlikely, given the wide-ranging philosophies that underpin this approach, that a definitive model will ever be agreed.

96

THE BRITISH SCHOOL OF EXISTENTIAL THERAPY

A number of practitioners and thinkers have made significant contributions to the practice of existential therapy without securing a particularly high profile outside the British group. Among these are Eugene Gendlin and Greg Madison (Focusing), Tim Lebon (philosophical counselling), Simon du Plock (working with addictions), Freddie and Alison Strasser (time-limited existential therapy), and R.D. Laing, who challenged the accepted tenets of psychiatry on the treatment of mental illness. However, the British School, as it is sometimes called, can be most readily identified in the works of the practitioners and authors who have had the greatest influence on the relatively new paradigm of existential and existential-phenomenological psychotherapy: Emmy van Deurzen, Ernesto Spinelli and Hans Cohn (Cooper, 2003).

The history of formal training for existential practice in the United Kingdom began with Regent's College, London (now Regent's University), where the School of Psychotherapy and Counselling was founded and developed by Emmy van Deurzen in 1982. Ernesto Spinelli joined the college faculty in 1989, and Hans Cohn was engaged at about the same time. All three have published texts and edited books throughout the subsequent decades, and their contributions to the field are widely read around the world.

Although each of these leaders came from varied backgrounds – philosophy, psychology and psychoanalysis – they share some common ground in terms of basic existential concepts: they all agree that there is no 'real' or essential self; they eschew intra-psychic models of the mind, and view life as fundamentally relational; they share the view that many of life's difficulties are a product of how we engage with the givens of existence. There are also shared philosophical affinities: van Deurzen references a broad range of sources, but acknowledges in particular the contributions of Jean Paul Sartre, Maurice Merleau-Ponty, F. Nietzsche, Martin Heidegger, and Soren Kierkegaard; Spinelli is more grounded in phenomenological thought, both classic and contemporary (though Cohn notes that 'all existential psychotherapy has a phenomenological dimension' (Cohn, 1997, p16)), but acknowledges the importance of many of the existential philosophers cited by van Deurzen; and Cohn is known for his scholarly appreciation of Martin Heidegger's works.

The divergence of these scholars and practitioners is more evident in their approaches to practice: van Deurzen is more pedagogical than the others; Spinelli is more collaborative in his enquiry; and Cohn demonstrates a preference for immediacy and extemporaneous dialogue, a reflection of his stance that existential therapy is a philosophical attitude rather than a paradigm for therapy.

The British School continues to develop and thrive, and its influence has generated extensive discussion and a growing appreciation of existential ideas and psychotherapeutic practice on a worldwide scale.

97

THE EUROPEAN SCHOOL OF EXISTENTIAL THERAPY

The European school is dominated by the models of Dasein-analysis and Logotherapy. Both are developments of the twentieth century that contain roots and practices from earlier approaches (particularly those of Freudian origins), although these are greatly modified.

Logotherapy is an approach that emphasises humans' ability to find meaning in even the most challenging circumstances. The word *logos* is of Greek origin, and is translated roughly as 'meaning' or 'concept' (Deurzen, 1997).

Although the texts of Frankl (the originator of Logotherapy) bear little reference to philosophical thinkers, his proposals that freedom is exercised in our attitude towards events and facts, and that we are meaning-seeking entities, are reminiscent of many of the themes found in existential works.

Additionally, Frankl proposes that we need a purpose in life, an aspiration or moral ambition that draws us towards our future. This notion is also similar to Sartre's ideas concerning projects and values.

Frankl was a survivor of the Holocaust. It is purported that his basic principles were formulated prior to this experience, and that the suffering he and others endured, and the meaning they took from these trials, served to substantiate his premises (Cooper, 2003).

His written works are very accessible, free of the difficult terminology sometimes found in philosophical and psycho-therapeutic texts. He incorporates a few techniques that have been adopted by practitioners, most notably 'paradoxical intention', in which the 'patient' is encouraged to exaggerate or exacerbate the very symptoms they are trying to avoid. In this manner they may recognise the part they play in creating the anxiety that attends these difficulties.

In general, the style of interaction between client and therapist might be described as somewhat directive, but this has been modified in more contemporary practices.

Daseinanalysis is founded primarily on the work of Martin Heidegger. The origin of the term is the seminal text of Heidegger, who designated human beings as 'Dasein', or 'being-there', or more specifically understood as 'the there of being' (Cohn, 1997). Binswanger emphasised a phenomenological approach founded on Edmund Husserl's tenets, a divergence, among others, which fostered a difference in thinking and practice between himself, Medard Boss and Heidegger.

Medard Boss, a Swiss psychoanalyst, entered into a friendship with Heidegger (1947/2000), and subsequently became instrumental in illuminating the later work of the philosopher in its relevance for psychotherapy. He, too, referred to his approach as Daseinanalysis, but owing in part to the direct influence of Heidegger, his style of working was more closely aligned with the principles of the philosopher.

Both proponents of this way of working share common goals with respect to the therapeutic endeavour: to help the client understand *how* they exist in the world, and the ways they close themselves off, or open themselves up, to various aspects of living. The therapist facilitates an exploration that allows the client to become more aware of how they participate in their own existence, and in what ways they curtail, and exercise, their freedom. These enquiries consider past experiences, as well as any physical ailments or symptoms. By virtue of these attitudes and enquiries, pathologies are seen as impairments or impediments to possibilities, and symptoms indicate unacknowledged and ineffective responses to the givens of existence.

98

THE NORTH AMERICAN SCHOOL OF EXISTENTIAL THERAPY

There has been active inter-play between the American take on existential ideas and the British and European Schools of existential philosophy and psychotherapy.

Rollo May and his associates James Bugental, Irvin Yalom and Kirk Schneider were all influenced by May's studies with philosopher and theologian Paul Tillich (Cooper, 2003). The approach that has come to be known as existential/humanistic was developed and maintained by these figures, and is a current part of the landscape of North American psychology and psychotherapy.

Common to the positions of these and related humanistic theorists like Abraham Maslow and Carl Rogers is an appreciation that many of life's problems stem from anxiety about the aspects of existence recognised in existential literature: finitude, death, responsibility, meaninglessness, freedom and relatedness. In an effort to deny or evade full acknowledgement of these factors, individuals may erect defences that they hope will protect them from a full appreciation of the implications of any or all of these. These defences can inhibit the development of an individual's potential, and curtail the innate life force that strives for realisation.

This proposal serves to illuminate some fundamental differences between the European and British Schools of thought and practice and the American School: there is a distinct emphasis on individualism in the latter (as opposed to the inter-relational character of life) as reflected in much of American culture; and there is an affinity for the idea that humans have innate potential for positive development and growth.

With respect to this emphasis, May (1969, p79) writes about the nature of 'insight' gained in therapy:

> the possibility of in-sight, of 'inward sight', of seeing the world and his problems in relation to himself.

The client is encouraged to look *within* for the source of their distress: they are only secondarily invited to consider how their place in the world, and how they helped to position themselves there, is entwined with their difficulties.

In this latter principle, the American School takes a position diametrically opposed to that of Sartre: in the American view, essence precedes existence. A further implication to this view is that there is little agreement with the tenet that humans create themselves in their choices.

Additionally, the proponents of the American perspective have a great affinity with the psychodynamic model of intra-psychic dynamics and mechanisms, and will refer to unconscious processes and forms of projection and transference. In this regard, they differ from the British and European schools in their respect for the human being as a unified whole, with the possibility of aspects becoming foreground or background.

In keeping with an individualistic and intra-psychic approach, humanistic-existential practitioners propose that there exists for or in each person a 'true' self, an entity that calls for realisation, actualisation and recognition. Again, this is in direct opposition to the philosophical concept that we find our selves in constant and changing interaction with others and our world.

The anomaly in this landscape is the school of thought developed by Betty Cannon, one of the world's foremost Sartrean scholars and former student and friend of Sartrean translator and scholar, Hazel E. Barnes. Cannon promotes an 'experiential psychodynamic' approach that is grounded in the works of Jean-Paul Sartre. Her seminal work, *Sartre and Psychoanalysis: An Existentialist Challenge to Clinical Metatheory* (1991), provides an account of psychotherapy based upon an in-depth appreciation of Sartre's work, and is currently practiced as AEP, or Applied Existential Psychotherapy.

99

EXISTENTIALISM AND OTHER THERAPEUTIC ORIENTATIONS

The theories that underpin most therapeutic orientations are founded on some form of philosophical understanding of the human condition. These philosophies address many of the same questions: What informs behaviour? What is the nature of emotional experience? What is the role of cognitive processes? What is knowledge? How much freedom, if any, do we have in making choices? What is truth? How does one live, and love?

How these kinds of questions are entertained, or answered, will inform how the therapist hears their clients' stories, and the way they respond to their clients' dilemmas. If the practitioner aligns himself or herself genuinely with the perspective they adopt, there should be no discrepancy between the theory and the practice: a philosophy of the human condition should pertain to everyone, in all circumstances.

It seems unlikely that an eclectic position with reference to theory and practice will be cohesive if the philosophies represented in these theories are not already fundamentally compatible. Examples of this might be those models that are fundamentally psychodynamic or cognitive behavioural. In any case, any paradigm that is applied needs to be considered for its essential proposals, to ensure that the particular approach employed by the practitioner is not impeded by contradictory assumptions.

Existential psychotherapy stands as a unique and cohesive approach, though its practice will manifest in a variety of permutations. This is due in large part to the idea that existentialism is an attitude: a *lived* philosophy, rather than an applied model. As such, therapists will share a common understanding of the human condition, and will engage in an exploration of the clients' experience as this understanding relates to them specifically.

Although this latter intention may be shared by other models, the existential therapist will be more concerned with 'being' qualities of the relationship, as opposed to the application of skills. This is more than an inter-relational analysis – it is an inter-subjective phenomenon. As a result, the quality of the situation and the relationship is co-constituted by all those involved, as well as by the entire world context.

The existential practitioner does not aim for solutions, or treatment, but understanding: both therapist and client, it is hoped, will come to a deeper, if not final, appreciation of the client's worldview.

Perhaps most significantly, existential therapists consider the future to be the temporal aspect of most concern: we are not determined by our past, though we are affected by it in ways that are particular to each of us; rather, we are pulled into our future by our aspirations and expectations, towards that finality that concludes our existence.

Finally, existential philosophy views people as free agents, albeit this freedom is always contextualised: choices and behaviour are always the effects of this freedom, rather than unconscious drives or motivations. Similarly, emotions are deemed to be informative, indicators of one's values and the assumptions underpinning the worldview: they are not the consequences of historical situations, nor would they ever be considered 'irrational' or 'inappropriate'.

The existential attitude remains intact as a unique attitude towards life and the therapeutic project.

100

THE CASE FOR EXISTENTIALISM AS AN OVER-ARCHING FRAMEWORK

There are few, if any, models of psychotherapy, or psychology, that can claim to possess a general relevance to any and every culture, across all époques, the way existentially based thought and practice can. As it addresses the issues that are of concern to every society and era, e.g. temporality, life and death, uncertainty, suffering and satisfaction, relationship, and freedom, its principles are central to any ethical and moral project.

In describing a fundamental aspect of existential philosophy, a philosophy that he describes as a *style* of philosophising, Macquarrie (1972, p14) states that 'it begins from man rather than from nature. It is a philosophy of the subject rather than of the object'. This proposal indicates that the consideration of how to live begins with each individual; it is a question that is answered by each in the particulars of their existence: it is not simply a rhetorical question.

However, as every individual is always part of a greater whole, their engagement with the concerns of life always have repercussions for the greater context: we are never alone. The individual and their community are inextricably bound.

In his anthology of readings in Western philosophy, Friedman (1992) refers to existential philosophy as a *temper* and a *mood,* as opposed to a systemised order of thought. To emphasise this inclusive principle, he declares that 'The root of existentialism is, of course, "existence"' (Friedman, 1992, p6). This proposal indicates that the arena for considering how to live lies not in theoretical abstraction, as useful as such analyses might be, but rather in the exploration of how any particular human being concretises their values and aspirations within their own existence, which is in turn situated within ever-expanding contexts.

Existential psychotherapy, focusing as it does on both the general, that is, the givens of existence, and the particular, that is how any particular person engages with the givens, is an enterprise that serves to elucidate the worldview of those who choose to enter into this project.

As an attitude, or temper or mood, the existential perspective can inform the enquiry into our behaviour, choices, situated freedom, aspirations for the future, the understanding of ourselves, and the conditions of relationship. These are concerns central to any therapeutic paradigm.

Where change is desired, it can be very effective to consider the meanings and values associated with the current situation, to discover what benefits and liabilities may be the effect of the change: in taking this approach, it may become clear what assumptions support the current situation, as these, too, are part and parcel of a difficult decision. As has often been suggested, change is the aim of the therapeutic process – though it may be a change in attitude rather than a change in behaviour.

How these kinds of enquiries are realised in practice may be varied, and will reflect the particulars of skills and strategies adopted by the practitioner. Supported by an appreciation of the existential givens that are common to all people, these explorations can effect a profound appreciation of our situation in the world, and how we exist in it.

REFERENCES

Adams, M. (2013) *Existential counselling*. London, Sage.

Barnett, L. (2008) *When death enters the therapeutic space: existential perspectives in psychotherapy and counselling*. Oxford, Routledge.

Barnett, L. (2009) *When death enters the therapeutic space*. London, Routledge.

Barrett, W. (1962/1990) *Irrational man*. New York, Anchor Books.

Becker, E. (1973) *The denial of death*. New York, Free Press Paperbacks.

Binswanger, L. (1963) *Being in the world: selected papers of Ludwig Binswanger*. New York, Basic Books.

Blackham, H.J. (1952/1978) *Six existential thinkers*. London, Routledge and Kegan Paul Ltd.

Boss, M. (1963) *Psychoanalysis and Daseinanalysis*. New York, Basic Books.

Boss, M. (1979) *Existential foundations of medicine and psychology*. New York, Jason Aronson.

Bracken, P. (2002) *Trauma, culture, meaning and philosophy*. London and Philadelphia, Whurr.

Buber, M. (2013) *I and thou*. London, Bloomsbury Academic.

Bugental, J. (1978) *Psychotherapy and process*. Reading, MA, Addison-Wesley.

Bugental, J.F.T. (1987) *The art of the psychotherapist: how to develop the skills that take psychotherapy beyond science*. New York, Norton.

Bugental, J.F.T. (1992) *The art of the psychotherapist: how to develop the skills that take psychotherapy beyond science*. New York, W.W. Norton & Company.

Camus, A. (1942) *Myth of Sisyphus* (J. O'Brien, 1955, trans). London, Penguin.

Camus, A. (1955/2000) *The myth of Sisyphus*. London, Penguin Books.

Cannon, B. (1991) *Sartre and psychoanalysis: an existential challenge to clinical metatheory*. Lawrence, KN, University Press of Kansas.

Cohn, H.W. (1997) *Existential thought and therapeutic practice: an introduction to existential psychotherapy*. London, Sage.

Cohn, H.W. (2002) *Heidegger and the roots of existential therapy*. London, Continuum.

Cooper, D. (1967) *Psychiatry and anti-psychiatry*. London, Tavistock.

Cooper, M. (2003) *Existential therapies*. London, Sage.

Cooper, M. (2012) *The existential counselling primer*. Ross-on-Wye, PCCS Books.

Corey, G. (2009) *Theory and practice of counselling and psychotherapy*. Belmont, CA, Brooks/Cole, Cengage.

Crowell, S. (2010) Existentialism. *Stanford Encyclopedia of Philosophy*. Available at: http://plato.stanford.edu/entries/existentialism (accessed 5 July 2013).

De Beauvoir, S. (1948) *The ethics of ambiguity*. Trans B. Frechtman. London, Citadel Books.

Deurzen, van, E. (1997) *Everyday mysteries: Existential dimensions of psychotherapy*. Oxford, Routledge.

Deurzen, van. E. (1998) *Paradox and passion in psychotherapy*. Chichester, Wiley.

Deurzen, van, E. (2002) *Existential psychotherapy in practice*. London, Sage.

Deurzen, van, E. (2007) 'Existential therapy' in W. Dryden, *Handbook of individual therapy*. London, Sage

Deurzen, van, E. (2008) *Psychotherapy and the quest for happiness*. London, Sage.

Deurzen, van, E. (2012) *Existential psychotherapy and counselling in practice*. London, Sage.

Deurzen, van, E., & Adams, M. (2010) *Skills in existential counselling and psychotherapy*. London, Sage.

Deurzen, van, E., & Arnold-Baker, C. (2005) *Existential perspectives on human issues*. Hampshire, Palgrave Macmillan.

Deurzen, van, E., & Iacovou, S. (2013) (eds) *Existential perspectives on relationship therapy*. Basingstoke, Palgrave Macmillan.

Deurzen, van. E., & Kenward, R. (2005) *Dictionary of existential psychotherapy and counselling*. London, Sage.

Deurzen, van, E., & Young, S. (2009) *Existential perspectives on supervision: Widening the horizon of psychotherapy and counselling*. London, Palgrave Macmillan.

Deurzen-Smith, van, E. (1995) *Existential therapy*. London, Society for Existential Analysis.

Du Plock, S. (2005) An existential-phenomenological critique of philosophical counselling. *Existential Analysis* 16 (1): 249–258.

Du Plock, S. (2013) Therapy with couples presenting with issues of addiction, in E. van Deurzen & S. Iacovou (eds), *Existential perspectives on relationship therapy*. London, Sage.

Evans, R.I. (1981) *Dialogue with R.D. Laing*. New York, Praeger.

Farber, L. (2000) *The ways of the will: selected essays*. New York, Basic Books.

Fingarette, H. (1998) *Heavy drinking, the myth of alcoholism as a disease*. Berkeley, CA, University of California Press.

Finlay, L. (2011) *Phenomenology for therapists*. Chichester, John Wiley & Sons.

Foucault, M. (1971) *Madness and civilisation*. London, Routledge.

Frankl, V. (1980) *Man's search for meaning*. New York, Simon and Schuster.

Frankl, V. (2004) *Man's search for meaning*. Reading, Rider.

Freud, S. (2013) *The unconscious*. New York, Tree of Knowledge.

Friedman, M. (1992) *The worlds of existentialism: a critical reader*. Atlantic Highlands, NJ, Humanities Press International.

Giorgi, A. (ed.) (1985) *Phenomenology and psychological research*. Pittsburgh, Duquesne University Press.

Goffman, E. (1961) *Asylums: essay on the social situation of mental patients and other inmates*. New York, Anchor Books.

Gordon, P. & Mayo, R. (2004) *Between psychotherapy and philosophy*. London, Whurr.

Griffiths, C., Norton, L., Wagstaff, G., et al. (2002). Existential concerns in late stage cancer. *European Journal of Oncology Nursing*, 6: 243–246.

Guigon, C.B. (2002) Existentialism, in *Routledge Encyclopedia of Philosophy*. Available at: www.rep.routledge.com (accessed 7 July 14).

Heaton, J. (2009) Reflections on suicide and despair, in L. Barnett (ed.) *When death enters the therapeutic space*. Hove, Routledge.

Heidegger, M. (1927) *Being and time*. (J. MacQuarrie and E. Robinson trans). London, Harper and Row, 1962.

Heidegger, M. (1947/2000) *Letters on humanism*. Edinburgh, Edinburgh University Press.

Heidegger, M. (1962) *Being and time*. (J. MacQuarrie and E. Robinson trans). Oxford, Blackwell.

Heidegger, M. (1978) *Being and time*. Chichester, Wiley Blackwell.

Heidegger, M. (2003) *Plato's sophist*. Bloomington, IN, Indiana University Press.

Husserl, E. (1931) *Cartesian meditations*. Trans. D. Cairns (1960). Dordrecht, Kluwer.

Husserl, E. (1936) *Die Krisis der europaischen Wissenschaften und die transzendentale phanomenologie: Eine Einleitung in die phanomenologiische philosophie.* Belgrade, Philosophia 1 .

Husserl, E. (2001 [1900/1901]). *Logical investigations.* Edited by Dermot Moran. 2nd ed. 2 vols. London, Routledge.

Iacovou, S. (2011) What is the difference between existential and so called neurotic anxiety? *Journal of Existential Analysis,* 22 (2): 356–367.

Jaspers, K. (1986) *Karl Jaspers: basic philosophical writings.* Trans. E. Ehrlich, L.H. Ehrlich & G.B. Pepper. Atlantic Highlands, NJ, Humanities Press International.

Jastrow Jr, M., & Clay, A.T. (2010) *The epic of Gilgamesh.* Los Angeles, CA, IndoEuropean Publishing Ltd.

Kaufman, W. A., & Nietzsche, F. (1974) *Philosopher, psychologist, antichrist.* Princeton, NJ, Princeton University Press.

Kierkegaard, S. (1844) *Philosophical fragments* (H.V. Hong and H.E. Hong trans. 1962). Princeton, NJ, Princeton University Press.

Kierkegaard, S. (1849/1980) *The sickness unto death* (H.V. Hong and H.E. Hong trans. 1980). Princeton, NJ, Princeton University Press.

Kierkagaard, S. (1944) *The concept of dread.* Trans. W. Lowrie. Princeton, NJ, Princeton University Press.

Kubler-Ross, E. (1969) *On death and dying.* New York, Scribner.

Laing, R.D. (1960) *The divided self: an existential study in sanity and madness.* Harmondsworth, Penguin.

Laing, R.D. (1961) *The self and others.* London, Tavistock Publications.

Laing, R.D. (1967) *The politics of experience and the bird of paradise.* Harmondsworth, Penguin.

Laing, R.D. (1969) *Self and others.* London, Penguin.

Laing, R.D. and Cooper, D.G. (1964) *Reason and violence: a decade of Sartre's philosophy.* 2nd ed. London: Tavistock Publications Ltd.

Lee, V. & Loiselle, C.G. (2012) The salience of existential concerns across the cancer control continuum. *Palliative and Supportive Care* 10 (2): 1–10.

Leontiev, D. (2013) The challenge of others: relationships, meaning and dialogue, in E. van Deurzen & S. Iacovou (eds) *Existential perspectives on relationship therapy: a guide for practice.* Basingstoke, Palgrave MacMillan.

Lester, S. (1999) *An introduction to phenomenological research.* Taunton, Stan Lester Developments. Available at: www.sld.demon.co.uk/resmethy.pdf (accessed 30 April 2014).

Macquarrie, J. (1972) *Existentialism.* Harmondsworth, Penguin.

Manen, van, M. (1997) *Researching lived experience: human science for an action sensitive pedagogy*. Winnipeg, Hignall Book Printing.

Marcel, G. (1949) *Being and having*. Trans. K. Farrer. London, Dacre Press.

May, R. (1969) *Existential psychology*. New York, McGraw-Hill.

May, R., Angel, E. & Ellenberger, H.F. (1958) *Existence*. New York, Jason Aronson.

Merleau-Ponty, M. (1962) *The phenomenology of perception*. Trans. C. Smith. London, Routledge.

Montaigne, M. de (1958) *Essays*. Trans. J.M. Cohen. London, Penguin Books.

Nietzsche, F. (1967) *Thus spake Zarathustra*. Trans. T. Common. London, Allen and Unwin.

Polt, R. (1999) *Heidegger, an introduction*. London, UCL Press.

Rank, O. (1929/1978) *Truth and reality*. London, Norton.

Rees, W.D. (1971) The hallucinations of widow-hood. *British Medical Journal*, 4, 37–41.

Rothschild, B. (2000) *The body remembers: the psychophysiology of trauma and trauma treatment*. New York, Norton Professional.

Sartre, J.P. (1943) *Being and nothingness: An essay on phenomenological ontology*. (H.E. Barnes, trans 1958). London, Meuthen.

Sartre, J.P. (1944) *No exit*. New York, Vintage Books.

Sartre, J.P. (1948/1973) *Existentialism and humanism*. Trans. P. Mairet. London, Methuen Publishing.

Sartre, J.P. (1955) *No exit and three other plays*. New York, Knof Doubleday.

Sartre, J.P. (1991) *The transcendence of the ego: a theory of consciousness*. London, Hill & Wang.

Savery, D. (2013) The challenges of meaningless and absurdity addressed through myth and role play, in E. Deurzen & S. Iacovou (eds) *Existential perspectives on relationship therapy*. London, Sage.

Schneider, K. (1999) *The paradoxical self: towards an understanding of our contradictory nature*. New York, Humanity Books.

Seamon, D. (2000) A way of seeing people and place: phenomenology in environment–behavior research, in S. Wapner, J. Demick, T. Yamamoto & H. Minami (eds) *Theoretical perspectives in environment–behavior research*. New York, Plenum Press.

Shakespeare, W. (2012) *As you like it*. London, Create Space Individuality Publishing Platform.

Smith, D.B. (2007) *Muses, madmen and prophets: rethinking the history, science and meaning of auditory hallucinations*. London, Penguin Books.

Smith, J.A. (2011) Evaluating the contribution of interpretative phenomenological analysis. *Health Psychology Review*, 5, 9–27.

Smith, J.A., Flowers, P. & Larkin, M. (2009) *Interpretative phenomenological analysis*. London, Sage.

Smith-Pickard, P. (2009) The experience of working with patients with a short prognosis, in L. Barnett (ed.) *When death enters the therapeutic space*. Hove, Routledge.

Spinelli, E. (1989) *The interpreted world: An introduction to phenomenological psychology*. London, Sage.

Spinelli, E. (1994) *Demystifying therapy*. London, Constable.

Spinelli, E. (2003) *Existential therapies*. London, Sage.

Spinelli, E. (2005) *The interpreted world*. London, Sage.

Spinelli, E. (2006) *Tales on the unknowing: therapeutic encounters from an existential perspective*. Ross-on-Wye, PCCS Books.

Spinelli, E. (2007) *Practising existential therapy: the relational world*. London, Sage.

Stolorow, R.D. (2007) *Trauma and human existence*. New York, Analytic Press.

Strasser, F., & Randolph, P. (2004) *Mediation: a psychological insight into conflict resolution*. London, Bloomsbury.

Strasser, F., & Strasser, A. (1997) *Existential time limited therapy*. London, John Wiley & Sons.

Suri, R. (2010) Hearing voices: what can we learn from them. *Psychosis*, 2 (2): 178–180.

Szasz, T. (1960) The myth of mental illness. *American Psychologist* 15 (2): 113–118.

Tallis, R. (2011) *Aping mankind*. Durham, Acumen Publishing.

Tanner, M. (1994) *Nietzsche*. Oxford, Oxford University Press.

Tantam, D. (2002) *Psychotherapy and counselling in practice: a narrative framework*. Cambridge, Cambridge University Press.

Tillich, P. (1952/1980) *The courage to be*. New Haven, CT and London, Yale University Press.

Tillich, P. (2000) *The courage to be*. New Haven, CT, Yale University Press.

Toledo, R.D. (2011) Existentialism and Latin America, in F. Joseph, J. Reynolds & A. Woodward (eds) *The Continuum companion to existentialism*. London, Continuum International Publishing Group.

Wahl, B. (2003) Working with 'existence tension' as a basis for existential practice. *Existential Analysis* 14 (2): 265–278.
Warnock, M. (1970) *Existentialism*. Oxford, Oxford University Press.
Wong, T.P. (2013) *The human quest for meaning: theories, research and applications*. New York, Routledge.
Yalom, I. (1980) *Existential psychotherapy*. New York, Basic Books.
Yalom, I. (2006) *The gift of therapy: reflections on being a therapist*. London, Piatkus.
Yalom, I. (2011) *Staring at the sun: overcoming the dread of death*. London, Piatkus.